MOUNTAINEERING
FOR ALL

RICHARD GILBERT

MOUNTAINEERING FOR ALL

B.T. Batsford Ltd, London

Diagrams by Dominic Elwes,
Andrew Hawkswell and Declan Morton.

All the unacknowledged photographs are
from the author's collection.

First published 1981
© Richard Gilbert 1981

ISBN 0 7134 3350 7

Filmset in Monophoto Baskerville by
Servis Filmsetting Ltd., Manchester

Printed in Great Britain by
The Anchor Press, Tiptree, Essex
for the publishers B.T. Batsford Ltd,
4 Fitzhardinge Street, London W1H 0AH

Contents

Introduction

My love of mountains goes back a very long way for I was lucky to have parents who walked and climbed in the hills at every opportunity. It was their relaxation and way of life and, from an early age, I and my twin brothers Oliver and Christopher had to come too because we could not be left behind.

Many and varied are the ways in which climbers have started their mountaineering careers. It does not take much to spark off an involvement with mountains that can bring a lifetime of pleasure. A film, television programme, book, school outing, adventure holiday or a conversation can provide the initial stimulus.

I was just two years old when the war started and we moved from London to the tiny village of Borth-y-gest on the very edge of Snowdonia in north Wales. Favourite outings and picnics were always to the hills, and the smell of bracken and heather, and the feel of rough rocks became familiar and symptomatic of carefree days. At the end of the war we moved back to London and mountain holidays with our parents were restricted to once or twice a year. This was too seldom for us because other pursuits such as rugby and Boy Scouts seemed tame compared with mountaineering. We poured scorn on those friends who took their holidays on the Costa Brava, for those early years in north Wales had given us a love of the hills which was to remain with us all our lives.

We longed for the family holidays in the hills of Britain or abroad and these were the highlights of our lives. Equipment was minimal but it did not seem to matter. Ex-Army gas capes, which ballooned up in the wind, sufficed against the rain and I remember climbing Great Gable through snow so deep that it came over the top of my wellingtons. In the Pyrénées we crossed the Brèche glacier to reach the Brèche de Roland above Gavarnie wearing only sandals and carrying sticks instead of ice axes.

During my last three years at school I hitch-hiked to the mountains during every school holiday, either with friends or with my brothers. North Wales at Christmas, Scotland at Easter and the Lake District in the summer became the regular pattern. Those years when we made all the decisions ourselves, read the maps and compass, selected the routes and equipment, and cooked our own meals, undoubtedly gave us confidence and most valuable experience of mountains under all conditions. The winter holidays were the most memorable. After hitching up the old A5 we would stay in a ramshackled cottage at Gwastadnant in the Llanberis Pass, rented for one shilling a night. We explored the Glyders, Tryfan and Y-Garn, slid on the frozen lakes and one fantastic day completed the Snowdon Horseshoe in full winter conditions.

I remember that day well for none of us knew the way along the knife-edged ridge from Snowdon summit to Crib Goch or the descent route to the road. It was misty and the January afternoon was drawing in as we scrambled and straddled our way along the ridge, there was no escape route and we were thoroughly committed. Finally frozen and rather frightened we managed to force a descent from Crib Goch, sliding from stone to stone as they stuck up through the icy slopes. But how proud and important we felt when, later that night at the Pen-y-Gwryd Hotel, Chris Briggs, the proprietor and Mountain Rescue Leader, told us that in the present conditions the route warranted the use of ice axes and a rope. Of course we had neither.

At about the same time that we were walking over the Welsh mountains the sport of rock climbing was making one of its periodic leaps forward led by Joe Brown and Don Whillans.

To us schoolboys, rock climbers were a world apart and we watched in wonder as they uncoiled their ropes and, shouting to each other in unintelligible jargon, started to move up the precipitous faces.

Rock climbing in the 1950s was a good deal simpler than it is today. Few, if any, climbers wore helmets or harnesses while nuts and artificial chocks were unknown. Nevertheless, there were many vital safety techniques to be learned and my parents wisely packed us off for a week's course at the Plas-y-Brenin Climbing Centre in north Wales. My instructor was the Olympic athlete John Disley and he worked us hard. By the end of the week we were climbing classic routes up to Severe standard and occasionally we were allowed to lead an easy pitch. Without nut runners some of the pitches were quite serious and a 50-foot run out by the leader, with no intermediate protection, was common place; a situation unheard of today. Undoubtedly this made rock climbing more dangerous and it is significant that the total annual number of rock climbing accidents is not much greater today than twenty years ago in spite of the tremendous growth of the sport and the rise in standards.

My introduction to rock climbing coincided with a family move to Northumberland. This gave us the opportunity to rock climb on the Whinsill outcrop of Crag Lough on the Roman Wall and the gritstone Wanney's Crag. We spent many happy evenings pitting our skills against routes named aptly as Centurion, Squeezy Bill and Idiot's Delight. The Lake District too was within easy reach and we worked our way through the classics: Napes Needle on Gable, the New West climb on Pillar and Moss Ghyll on Scafell West Buttress. Two years' National Service in the Army necessarily curtailed my mountaineering activities but I managed a few 'stolen' climbs. The Tors on Dartmoor, winter climbing in the Cairngorms whilst (officially) on a skiing course, and a few trips to north Wales.

I will never forget one such expedition on a forty-eight-hour leave pass from Blandford Camp in Dorset. It was late November and I chugged up overnight through the Welsh borders on my BSA 125 c.c. motor bike. I met my brother Christopher at Capel Curig in pouring rain but we were determined to bag a few summits if nothing else. After sleet on the Glyders and hail on Bristly Ridge, we reached the summit of Tryfan in mid-afternoon just as the clouds were lifting. Below us in the valley the storm clouds were still lowering but on our high perch the sun was shining and we witnessed a magnificent Brocken Spectre. Our shadows appeared huge and menacing on the sea of clouds below, the outline of our bodies sparkling with rainbow colours. As we waved our arms the ghostly shadows mimicked us. I have seen the Brocken Spectre on several other occasions but never in such intensity as from Tryfan that November day.

In Great Britain the Mecca for rock climbers is the Cuillin range on the Isle of Skye. Straight after my demobilization Christopher and I hitched up to the Misty Isle for a week's climbing. Our final lift from Inverness to Dunvegan Castle was with Dame Flora Macleod of Macleod in her Rolls Royce. The holiday continued as well as it started and our climbs ranged from the Pinnacle Ridge of Sgurr nan Gillean to the Cioch Direct and Crack of Doom, on the famous cliff of Sron na Ciche, described in the guide book as the best climb in Skye.

I have always been a romantic and I find that Skye has everything to offer – black pointed peaks which rise straight out of the sea, sharp ridges enclosing blue lochs and from everywhere views of the islands of the Inner Hebrides with white breakers crashing on their shores. The rock is gabbro and its rough, tough nature is ideal for climbing. There are few easy days for the walker in the Cuillin and mountaineering, in all its forms, is required if the peaks are to be tackled safely.

Four years at university broadened my mountaineering experience. The stimulus of other dedicated mountaineers and a hint of competitiveness drove up my standard. The Mountaineering Club introduced me to the Alps and Dolomites and, nearer home, the pleasures of steep ice climbing on the north face of Ben Nevis and Lochnagar. I loved the delicate climbing on the limestone of the Avon Gorge at Bristol, a favourite cliff for a Sunday excursion, but I was less happy on the brutally

1 Milestone Buttress, Tryfan. An ideal crag for starting rock climbing. (Photograph by K. Wilson)

steep and overhanging gritstone outcrops of Derbyshire and Yorkshire.

As a contrast to hard rock and ice climbing I loved mountain walking and high camping in Scotland. The sheer beauty of the western Highlands in spring when the winter snows are still covering the high tops, the burns are brimming with melt water and the scrub birch and willow is coming into bud, cannot be bettered anywhere in the world.

In recent years I have introduced hundreds of boys to mountaineering and although not all of them have continued with the sport when they have left school, all have gained unique experiences which they can treasure for the rest of their lives.

The most difficult part of an introduction to the hills is the initial resistance. The popular view of mountaineering concentrates on the dangers inherent in the sport, the rock falls and avalanches, the cold and exposure. The layman fears the discomfort of being wet, frightened and exhausted; he sees walkers weighed down with huge packs, struggling and sweating along the roads, and he pities them. But such fears are groundless. Unless he wishes to use the mountains as a testing ground for his fitness he need not carry a huge load; if his ambitions are modest he need not expose himself to danger and if he has equipped himself correctly, cold and wet will not cause him discomfort.

Every mountaineer responds differently to the challenge of the hills and I hope that this book will persuade its readers to go out into the hills and sample the delights for themselves. Mountaineers are no longer regarded as eccentrics, they are privileged people having access to high and unspoilt country, a different world from the population centres and concrete jungle below.

It is a good idea for a prospective mountaineer to join his local climbing club where he will meet enthusiasts from all the different branches of the sport. Alternatively, if he does not enjoy the club atmosphere, he can start climbing with a friend – the choice is his entirely.

The instructions that I have given on hill walking, snow and ice climbing, rock climbing, equipment and navigation are sufficient for climbs of up to intermediate standard to be safely attempted.

1 Hill Walking

By ten o'clock the sun had just broken through the morning mist and the frost on the blades of grass was rapidly turning to dew. On the grey boulders the mica schist crystals were sparkling like diamonds. We had established a steady rhythm, one foot in front of the other, and although I was getting hot under my windproof anorak, I decided to bear it for a while longer because we were going so well. At the 1000-foot level we rounded an outcrop of rock and were brought up short by a piercing shriek. There right in front of us was a golden eagle at grips with a white mountain hare. The eagle's talons were firmly grasping the neck of the wretched animal and for a moment it turned its head and glared at us with yellow eyes before it released its prey and soared away towards Glen Lyon.

We were traversing the Ben Lawers range in central Perthshire and, although it was mid-April, spring comes late to the Scottish Highlands. The high corries were still packed with snow and cornices overhung the ridges. Although we carried ice axes they were for emergency use only, for we had no ambitious plans to attempt a steep gully or snow slope. We were hill walking and enjoying the complete freedom of choice which that activity affords.

The highest point of the day was reached at the 3984-foot summit of Ben Lawers and we sat down beside the cairn and ate a leisurely lunch. From our perch we could look down the full length of Loch Tay from Killin to Kenmore, the surface of the water showed barely a ripple and the willows on the banks were just tinged with green. The scrub birch trees on the lower slopes were in bud and the sunlight reflected brilliantly off the white bark. Smoke was rising from the hills above Glen Lyon as the estate workers took advantage of the dry spell to burn off some of the old heather. The southern slopes of Ben Lawers are a botanist's paradise and later in the year they would be ablaze with snow gentians, alpine forget-me-nots, speedwells, saxifrages and the pink moss campion.

As the afternoon wore on we traversed the outlying peaks of An Stuc and Meall Garbh and then walked back beside a rushing burn, swollen with melt water, to the glen and a good tea in Killin. It had been a glorious day of sheer indulgence, a day for the connoisseur. There had been no worries, no traumas and the pace had been leisurely. Hill walking is an activity which should be completely free from mental strain. It is a tonic to the tired and the overworked and it is the ideal complement to our stress-laden lives.

Almost anybody can become a hill walker, you don't need a lot of expensive equipment and you don't need to be a superman. What you do need is time, opportunity and motivation.

Why do we climb?

One's response to mountains must be subjective and the much quoted reply of George Mallory, 'Because it's there', is as good a reason as any. I believe that man has an innate driving force to seek challenge and to explore his planet. This driving force has taken many people to the mountains where they have discovered delights and rewards and they have eventually become mountaineers. Go out to the mountains yourself and I am confident that you will fall under their spell, you will soon grow to love them and a lifetime of pleasure will await you.

Accepting and striving to overcome a challenge is, for the human race, a very common pastime and intellectual exercise. Games, races, crossword puzzles and quizzes are all examples of activities where we like to 'have a go'. Likewise the challenge of mountaineering motivates many people to take up the sport. I defy anyone to go to Zermatt and gaze at the stupendous rock peak of the Matterhorn, towering 10,000 feet above the valley, and not feel an urge to try and climb it – an urge which led to the deaths of many men before Whymper succeeded in the attempt in 1865. Whymper wrote of the view from the summit, 'There was every combination of mountains that the world can give and every contrast that the heart could desire'. A few minutes later the rope broke and four of his companions plunged to their death down the north face.

Mountaineering is all about climbing to the tops of mountains but the climbs do not need to be difficult for them to be satisfying. Several years ago I set myself a target to ascend the 280 mountains in Scotland which are over 3000 feet. These peaks were first listed in 1891 by Sir Hugh Munro and they are known as the Munros. Sir Hugh died with two Munros still unclimbed and the first man to complete the list was A.E. Robertson in 1901. For ten years I spent almost all my spare time in the Highlands exploring every corner and remote glen and steadily knocking off the Munros. I was highly motivated and I lived for the weekends when I would drive north through the night to the next objective. Sir Hugh's attitude and example were a great inspiration to me. Remote mountains and bad weather were merely extra challenges to him, and if walking companions could not be found he would go alone. The occasion on which I climbed my final Munro, Bidean nam Bian in Glencoe, was one of the highlights of my life. We held a champagne party by the summit cairn and I felt more elated than after any hard rock climb or Alpine or Himalayan ascent.

The competitive aspect of hill walking takes many people to the mountains. We have the circuit of the fourteen Welsh 3000-foot peaks to be completed in a day, the Yorkshire three peaks, the Lakeland 3000-foot circuit and many others. Recently over 2000 hill walkers took part in a two-day mountain marathon over the southern uplands of Scotland. In these events the mountains are used as a testing ground for stamina, resourcefulness and map reading and I find them most enjoyable.

What I have little sympathy with, however, is the use of mountains for so-called leadership training. The hypothesis being that by bashing groups of young people carrying enormous rucksacks over the mountains in all weathers, latent qualities of guts, determination and leadership are brought out. The only result that it undoubtedly achieves is the instillation into the victims of a life-long, deep loathing for the hills.

By far the greatest proportion of hill walkers are motivated by the aesthetic pleasures of the mountains. The acceptance of mountains as being aesthetically pleasing has come only fairly recently. In the eighteenth century a traveller to the Highlands wrote of the hills, 'They are a dismal gloomy brown drawing upon a dirty purple and are most of all disagreeable when the heather is in bloom. The clearer the day, the more rude and offensive they are to the sight'. Even Dr Johnson wrote of the hills, 'The appearance is that of matter incapable of form or usefulness, dismissed by nature from her care and disinherited of her favours'. Queen Victoria on the other hand loved the romantic element of the Highland scene. She ascended a number of the major peaks and wrote in her diaries of her ascent of Ben Macdui, 'Never shall I forget this day, truly sublime and impressive, such solitude'.

Hill walking is a friendly sport, a family sport for young and old alike. Firm friendships are made on the hills and climbing clubs exist in most towns and cities where you can meet fellow mountaineers and recount past adventures, and plan new ones for the future. Another advantage of being a club member is that you can use the huts and cottages belonging to the club and often, by mutual agreement, those of other clubs as well. Climbing huts are usually set in the depths of the mountains and they cater exclusively for the needs of the climber. Good fires, plenty of hot water, drying rooms, bunk beds and large kitchens are provided at cost price and they are havens of warmth and comfort.

It may be that the actual hill walking process takes second place to another interest. Ornithologists, botanists, geologists and meteorologists will certainly venture into the mountains in the furtherance of their studies. If they are competent mountaineers as well they will be able to explore, in safety, a wider variety of mountain terrain. I was recently on the summit of Cairngorm (4084 feet) during an unpleasant squall of hail and I took shelter beside the huge cairn. To my surprise an aluminium aerial together with a wide variety of meteorological instruments rose out of the ground, remained exposed to the elements for a few minutes and then retreated back into the bowels of the Earth. It was a fully automatic remote controlled meteorological station installed by Edinburgh's Heriot-Watt University. I couldn't help but compare this device with the instruments on the summit of Ben Nevis (4406 feet), during the last century. Between 1 June and 1 November 1881 and again in 1882 Clement Wragge, a meteorologist, ascended Ben Nevis every single day. He would rise at 4.00 a.m., reach the summit at 9.00 a.m., make observations for two hours and return home by 3.00 p.m. He stopped only when a permanently staffed observatory was built.

All climbers should have some knowledge of the flora and fauna of the mountains for there is much for the trained eye to see that can enhance the enjoyment of a mountain walk. Choose your companions carefully though for I once undertook a long and arduous mountain traverse with a friend who was a lichenologist. He found many interesting specimens of lichen on the mountain summits which he wanted to take back for his students, but since the substratum was rock, and this had to come too, our rucksacks became very heavy indeed.

Hill walking is mountaineering in its broadest sense. You need a knowledge of map and compass, safety procedures, rudimentary rope work and snow and ice craft. The more skills you can develop the greater the number of hill walking options there will be open to you.

Even on easy hills there will be risks and you may find thrills and excitements when traversing narrow ridges or scrambling up steep rocks but, unlike rock climbing, the danger is not an integral part of the sport. At the beginning, while you are gaining experience in the hills, take particular care. Do not be too ambitious and if conditions should deteriorate, turn back at once. Statistics show quite clearly that the majority of mountain accidents happen to novices during their first few years of hill walking.

Choice of route

The choice of route is by far the most important decision of the day because so many variables are involved. Do not leave the decision until the last minute, sit down after supper the night before, scrutinize the map, take advice and make sure you have considered the following points.

1 The walk should have an aim, perhaps an attempt on a mountain summit, a horseshoe walk or a walk to a distant lake or waterfall. I find with children that a definite aim is important to keep up their interest and morale otherwise they quickly become bored and they drag behind well before they are tired. If you can motivate children you will find that they are full of energy and bounce, and they scramble up mountains with the ease of goats.

2 The walk should be as varied as possible. Try to get off the beaten track, explore some little-known area, the more adventurous the walk the more rewarding you will find it to be. If you can link sections of grass, rock scrambling, scree slopes, ridges and boulder fields and perhaps include a visit to a cliff face or a rocky gorge it will make for an all-round mountain day.

3 Plan well ahead and choose a sensible route. Remember that slopes of scree or soft snow are easy to descend but murder to ascend. Do not confront an inexperienced party with an exposed rock scramble or a steep icy slope late in the day when they are tired and more likely to make errors. Try and get most of the day's ascent done early while the party is still fresh. In wet weather be on your guard against difficult river crossings.

4 It is bad policy to split up a party and the pace of any group is dictated by that of the slowest member. Plan the route with this in mind and try to get to know the individual capabilities of your party.

5 Check the hours of daylight that are available to you and allow a safe margin. Always get down off a mountain well before dark even if the walk back to base through the valley has to be completed by torch light.

6 Distances measured from the map in hilly districts are notoriously misleading. For estimating time and distance use Naismith's

Rule. The rule allows a speed of 3 m.p.h. plus half an hour for every 1000 feet climbed. Note that the rule is for an average party in good weather. It does not include stops nor does it take into account load carrying, bad terrain, bad weather or fatigue at the end of the day. Remember too that when calculating actual ascent you must take account of undulating ground. Thus, if you ascend 500 feet, descend 400 feet, then ascend another 300 feet, the total ascent is 800 feet although you end up only 400 feet higher than your starting point. Naismith's Rule apart, for long uphill ascents a rate of 1500 feet per hour is good going.

2 Striding Edge on Helvellyn, one of the classic airy ridges of the Lake District. (Photograph by Tom Parker)

7 If you plan a walk across the mountains from one point to another point rather than a circular walk, make quite sure there is adequate transport to take you back to the start. There is nothing more depressing for a tired, cold, wet and hungry party of walkers than to have to hang around at the end of the day for a bus or, worse still, to be faced by a 10-mile walk back along the road. On the other hand, if you are able to finish the walk at a hotel bar you will undoubtedly motivate the older members of your party over the last few miles. If you are able to use two cars there is no problem because one car can be left at the finish of the walk to await your arrival.

The return to base after a long day's hill walking can be a most relaxing and satisfying journey. I once climbed the remote Ladhar Bheinn in the wilds of Knoydart in western Scotland and, after descending to the hamlet of Inverie on the south side, I returned to Mallaig by motor boat. Chugging back across the beautiful Loch Nevis in the glow of the sunset with the peak of Ladhar Bheinn outlined against the northern sky, secure in the knowledge that it had been conquered by a tough struggle, was a most satisfying and memorable experience.

8 Telephone for an up-to-date weather forecast and plan the length and height of the walk accordingly. It is a surprising fact that the air temperature drops 1°F for each 300 feet of ascent and the force of the wind increases proportionately. You will soon learn that a stiff wet breeze down in the valley changes to a howling blizzard of snow and sleet on the mountain tops. Likewise it is comforting to know that a sudden severe storm on the tops can be avoided by a quick descent to the shelter of the valley.

Mountaineers are very conscious of the weather and their eyes are continually scanning the horizons for layers of grey stratus clouds, the sure sign of an approaching front.

9 However confident you are about the strength and stamina of your party, accidents can happen. Sprained ankles, pulled muscles and other minor injuries can occur at any time and you should know the whereabouts of the escape routes down to lower ground.

10 Make sure that all members of the party have the right equipment for the route that you select. If you plan to go high during the winter months everyone must have ice axes and if the snow is likely to be hard and slippery they must have crampons too. If the route includes some rock climbing, however simple, you must carry a rope.

11 However closely you study the map there is no substitute for first-hand knowledge of the mountains. Advice from other climbers who know the area can be invaluable. They can tell you about changes in the land since the map was printed; perhaps certain hillsides have now been afforested or lakes dammed. They can guide you as to rights of way, bridges that are down, mountains that are magnetic and affect the compass and in a host of other ways.

On one most inauspicious occasion I was descending late in the day from a remote mountain. As I emerged below the clouds expecting to see a good track leading me home I was horrified to find a vast sheet of water and no path at all. A new hydro-electric scheme had raised the level of the loch and extended it three miles west, and the water had also submerged the path. I never made it back that night but had to survive a forced bivouac in extremely unpleasant conditions.

Moving over rough ground

Hill walking is very different to walking over flat ground. Not only must you contend with terrain that is steep but in all probability it will be rough and uneven, and it may be slippery and covered with loose boulders as well. Every footstep has to be carefully placed and this means looking down and working out exactly which line is the best one for you to take. It is much better not to follow the footsteps of the walker in front of you but to keep your distance and make your own decisions.

Even on the steepest ground there are always wrinkles, depressions, embedded rocks or tussocks of grass on which you can place your feet and thus keep upright, in perfect balance without too much strain on the ankles. The process is not nearly so difficult as it sounds and it soon becomes second nature. Almost without thinking you find yourself placing your feet flat on the steep hillside, carefully avoiding loose boulders, wet, slippery grass or verglassed rocks. It is quicker to climb steep ground on the toes but it is far more tiring and this method places a great strain on the ankle and calf muscles. You will find that zig-zagging from side to side is the most comfortable way of ascent.

Mountain paths make for easy, if unadventurous, walking and in popular areas such as the Lake District the mountains are criss-crossed with man-made paths. In Scotland too even quite remote mountains and glens have extremely well-constructed pony tracks, built by cheap labour during the last century, for stalking parties to gain easy access to the hills and to bring down the deer at the end of the day. Sheep paths are rarely much use to the hill walker. These narrow paths never seem to go in the right direction and they tend to contour round the mountains at certain fixed levels.

The key to walking uphill is rhythm. Your steps should be short and measured and your breathing regular; if your breath comes in gasps or your muscles are aching you are going too fast. Once you get into a rhythm, even a slow one, you will find that you are covering the ground surprisingly rapidly, easily and effortlessly. For this reason rests, which break rhythm, should be kept to an absolute minimum. Some stops of course are necessary but try to accomplish several tasks during the one pause. Let us suppose you are the leader and are forced to stop in order for some stragglers to catch up. Now is your chance to check the map, take a compass bearing, have a bite to eat, take off that extra sweater, tighten your laces and take a photograph. If you can find a large boulder or a wall to shelter behind during the rest, so much the better, because when you are not moving you will very quickly stiffen up and become cold.

If you slip while boulder hopping across a stream and get a boot full of water don't worry, it is not worth stopping for, because your foot will soon dry out and warm up. In winter, though, it would be worth wringing out your socks in order to prevent your foot becoming frozen. Likewise if your boots are rubbing and you can feel a blister forming you must stop immediately and take action. The nagging pain of a blistered heel is very wearing and it detracts completely from the day's pleasure.

Always remember that you are walking for fun so try to make the day's excursion as pleasant as possible. If you can get yourself fit before your walking holiday, by playing squash or jogging or some other energetic pursuit, you will reap the rewards. Not only will you be able to tackle the steepest slope with confidence but you will be able to cover more ground and have a correspondingly wider safety margin. If you are fit your mind can concentrate on the beauty of the surroundings rather than on the effort of placing one foot in front of the other. Besides, you will have breath to spare for talking to your friends.

Another important point to remember is not to carry too much on your back. Buy a small rucksack for yourself and get into the habit of always carrying your own things – a light rucksack is hardly felt. If you do share with others, the rucksack will be heavy and the straps will probably need adjustment at every swop-over. Bad feeling and resentment break out as you imagine your turn is the longest and the ground is more difficult than your partner's.

One of the most difficult things to accomplish in the mountains is keeping the right temperature. You will find that you tend to be uncomfortably hot when going uphill and too cold on the summits, and exposed ridges. This is why a wide variety of clothing should be taken. It is well worth a few seconds removing a sweater or pulling on an anorak.

Food is another question which is open to individual preference. Lack of food is very debilitating in the mountains and it is important to eat at regular intervals. Food should be appetizing to encourage you to eat, so feel free to indulge yourself with some of your favourite morsels. On a mountain walk I usually become dry throated so I take moist foods. Sandwiches with cheese and lots of chutney, jam sandwiches and moist rich fruit cake instead of biscuits are my favourites. Chocolate and glucose tablets really do revive a flagging body at the end of the day and they do not take up much room.

For lazy days I take a thermos flask of soup or tea and for days spent high up on the ridges I take a water bottle, otherwise I prefer to rely on streams for my drinking water and save the weight in my rucksack. A cup is useful to stop you getting wet knees when drinking from streams, and a spoonful of lemonade crystals stirred into a cup of water is most reviving. There is nothing nicer than ice-cold water from a spring or a patch of melting snow but be careful not to drink too much too quickly. I have known people suffer dreadful stomach pains through unthinkingly gulping down large volumes of icy water when they themselves were hot and sweaty.

3 Spring snow on Ingleborough, one of the famous Yorkshire Three Peaks. (Photograph by Tom Parker)

Many hill walkers whom I know find the descent from the mountains at the end of the day to be knee-jarring and unpleasant although, personally, I have never found this to be so. If the ground is hard you should keep your knees bent, thereby allowing the strong thigh muscles to take the strain. Once again place the feet flat on the ground and take a zig-zag route downhill. If the ground is waterlogged and soft or you are lucky enough to find a slope of runnable scree, you should adopt a more upright stance and dig your heels firmly into the ground.

Scree runs are banks of small stones which have built up over the years through erosion and rock fall from cliffs above. A good slope of scree maintains a precarious equilibrium and as you run down it the bank of stones moves down with you rather like a moving staircase.

The small stones cushion the feet and one can run down banks of scree at a great rate.

Scree running is an exhilarating sport but it has its dangers. Do not lose control and do not scree run with your companions in a straight line behind you. Larger boulders tend to bound down the slope and they could injure another member of the party. Descend at widely spaced intervals or in an arrow head formation. If a stone does break loose and starts rolling, give the rock climber's shout of 'Below!' to warn everyone of the danger. Make sure that the scree slope ends with a gentle run out and take particular care in misty weather.

A tragic accident happened to a school party several years ago in the Cuillin hills of Skye. After a misty day on the ridges the leader arrived at the top of a splendid scree slope. 'Bomb down here boys', the party was told, 'Coire Lagan is down below'. Unfortunately the scree slope was above the precipices of Coir' A' Ghrunnda and several of the party were killed.

4 In the Lyngen Range, Arctic Norway.

With more and more people taking to the hills most scree slopes have been run out and all that remains is a slope of jagged boulders or rough earth. But on your travels and explorations to remote regions you should be lucky enough to find some good scree runs. I know for sure that there are still hundreds in the High Atlas mountains of Morocco, in Iceland and in Arctic Norway. I know a few in Scotland too.

Hill walkers in summer and autumn will almost certainly come across heather-clad slopes. Heather is beautiful but misleading. From a distance it appears to cloak the lower slopes of the hills with a smooth purple blanket. But once in deep heather you will find that the going is tough and exhausting, the roots trip you up and the leaves cover hidden rocks and pot holes. Heather is best avoided.

It is often tempting, particularly in misty weather, to descend a mountain by following a stream. Unfortunately this is a very unwise move. Stream beds can be death traps because the water wears its way down to bed rock and carves out deep gullies and gorges, often with steps, waterfalls and cascades. If you are seeking a way down a mountain your best course of action is to find the place on the map where the contour lines are furthest apart and attempt to make your descent there.

Even if you are not the leader of your party I advise you to buy your own map and compass. Take an interest in the route, the names of the mountains, the compass bearing and the

decision making and you will enjoy the day all the more.

Once you have mastered the art of moving safely over mountainous country you have a wide choice of magnificent terrain to explore. You can go anywhere in your own country or you can travel abroad and walk in foreign mountain ranges. Both have their attractions. However well you know your local hills there will always be the changing conditions of weather and season that can transform their familiar appearance and degree of difficulty. Most hill walkers have their own favourite range of mountains, they return to them again and again to be reassured by their sameness, their unchangeability. My particular favourites are the Highlands of Scotland and my thoughts often turn to them during the day. After an early winter snowfall, a late spring frost or a soft day in autumn, I wonder what mood the mountains are in and I start scheming for a stolen weekend away in the north.

Sound experience of hill walking is the best possible stepping off point for graduation into rock climbing and advanced snow and ice climbing. It teaches you about mountain conditions, the types and textures of different rocks, balance and friction. When you have served your apprenticeship on the hills you are already a mountaineer and are well on the way to becoming a complete mountaineer.

2 Rock Climbing

Rock climbing is the king of sports. What other pastime can provide an exacting test of physical fitness, balance, cool-headedness and nerve combined with the excitement of exposure and the taste of fear? The heightened awareness and exhilaration is akin to the effect of a stimulant drug. In addition the feeling of well-being and satisfaction enjoyed on the completion of a rock climb is unique in my experience. Geoffrey Winthrop Young, the famous mountaineer and author wrote: 'The thrill of a mountain first seen or of a first climb attempted, remains for each newcomer a unique sensation'.

Do not be put off by the popular image of rock climbing as portrayed by the television spectaculars. Certainly there are exceptionally hard climbs up overhanging rocks and across vast sweeps of blank wall but these are for the expert. Every weekend thousands of climbers flock to cliffs and rock faces to swarm up the cracks, chimneys and buttresses of far easier routes. Rock climbing is not a dangerous sport if it is carried out correctly and, bearing in mind the experience of the party, the right route is selected.

Most rock faces abound with routes of all standards and are suitable for all tastes. Guide books to the cliffs indicate the grades and differing characters of the routes. They do not tell the reader how he should tackle the climb, nor do they indicate the position of the holds, but they are essential for the climber to be able to plan a suitable route. The climber does not want to find the way ahead blocked by a severe overhang or threatened by loose rock when he is nearing the top of the cliff.

Some knowledge and ability at rock climbing is essential for the all-round mountaineer who needs to be able to move safely over different kinds of mountainous terrain in all conditions. A few rock climbers, though, treat the sport as an end in itself and are quite content to drive their cars to the bottom of a convenient cliff where they climb hard routes all day. These purists are not interested in climbing to the tops of mountains or exploring remote valleys and ridges, and I think they miss much of the pleasure that a broader-based attitude to mountaineering provides. Perhaps the best mountaineering days of all are those which involve a degree of rock climbing such as the ascent of a steep rocky ridge finishing up at a mountain summit and then a long high walk back to the starting point.

Having the ability to tackle moderate rock routes increases the options open to the mountaineer. Many superlative routes at home and abroad need a degree of rock climbing expertise. The Cuillin ridge on Skye, Ben Nevis by the Tower Ridge and the Hörnli Ridge on the Matterhorn come to mind.

Rock climbing itself is a very simple exercise, it is the use of correct safety procedures that need to be learnt. It is difficult to explain to a person how he should climb a rock route, for most people like to do it their own way and, as in most sports, there is room for unconventionality and flair. To succeed on rock you do not even need to be tall or exceptionally strong. Climbers such as Joe Brown, Don Whillans and Peter Crew who have, in their time, pushed forward the standards of British rock climbing are all quite short men. Some of the best climbers today are women who use balance rather than brute strength to ascend a rock face.

Don't be put off rock climbing by exaggerated stories of bravado from the hard men. Don't be put off by vertigo; many rock climbers, myself included, suffer occasionally from vertigo. Vertigo can be conquered and the sight of the thick nylon rope snaking up in front of you is wonderfully reassuring.

5 Cornish granite. Terriers Tooth, Chair Ladder.
(Photograph by K. Wilson)

From a safety point of view it is essential to be
thoroughly acquainted with the use of a rope,
the technique of belaying and the abseil
method of descending a rock face. Ropes are
often carried for emergencies only and, if their
use is required, speed is of paramount
importance. There must be no fumbling with
coils of rope, slings or knots and no hesitation
in setting up safety ropes or abseils. Thus for
safety reasons alone a knowledge of the various
techniques in this chapter is important.

The principles of rope management

It is common misapprehension for laymen to
think that in a team of rock climbers it is only
the leader who actually climbs the rock and
the other members climb the rope! The rope is
only a safeguard and on the majority of climbs
it comes under no tension at all. A climber
who falls off a rock face and is held by the rope
has probably no business to be on that climb in
the first place. I feel strongly that falls should

not be taken lightly for they can put the safety
of the whole team in jeopardy. Falls may occur
through the ever-present objective dangers such
as stone fall or friable rock but I deplore the
increasing tendency amongst the few to push
themselves to, and occasionally beyond, the
limit. A fall whilst climbing should be a cause
for alarm and reflection, and should not be
accepted as a routine occurrence.

Exceptionally long and difficult climbs like
Bonington's attack on the south-west face of
Everest and Harlin's epic on the north face of
the Eiger in winter are tackled by a special
method. Here the leader climbs up to a stance,
belays himself and ties off the main climbing
rope. The second and subsequent climbers then
ascend the rope using sprung metal clamps,
called Jumars, which grip the rope. This
technique is used solely to force a climb and to
provide a safe method of retreat, for the fixed
rope runs all the way down the face, and its
use is restricted to expeditions geared to win a
summit at all costs. These are known as seige
tactics and are beyond the scope of this book.

Close examination of a rock face reveals

hundreds of climbing aids. Ledges, cracks, chimneys, bulges and hollows are all used by the rock climber to make his ascent. Few cliffs are truly vertical and every degree less than ninety makes for more friction and an easier route.

The leader ties on to one end of the main climbing rope and begins the ascent. The second man is belayed securely to a convenient rock at the base of the cliff and he pays out the climbing rope to the leader as required. He ensures that the rope runs smoothly and is free from snags, kinks and tangles.

As the leader works his way up the rocks he attaches running belays to act as safeguards in case he should fall. Running belays are loops of rope or nylon tapes which are fastened on to the rocks by a variety of methods. Alloy links called karabiners or 'krabs' are used to clip the main climbing rope to the running belay slings. The climbing rope can move easily inside the karabiner but if the leader should fall, the running belay prevents him from falling to the bottom of the cliff. He falls only twice the vertical distance that he was above the belay when the slip occurred. The second man takes the strain from below and lowers the leader to easier ground. The leader will put on as many running belays as possible so that he never gets too far away from the last one. A falling leader imparts a terrific strain both on the rope and on the second man, and sometimes the second is pulled upwards off his stance. This is why he should be belayed securely to the rock.

When the leader arrives at a convenient ledge or stance, usually after 60–100 feet of climbing, he belays himself to the rock and pulls in the slack rope. He has now completed the first stage or pitch of the climb and he can enjoy a well-earned rest.

The second man now starts climbing and as he proceeds up the rocks the leader takes in the slack and the third man pays out another rope linking him to the second. The second man should remove the leader's running belays unless he is on a traverse line, in which case he clips them on behind him to give himself protection from both front and rear. Such

6 More Cornish granite. Mitre route, Chair Ladder. The climber is Frank Cannings. (Photograph by K. Wilson)

protection was denied the leader and will be denied to the third man. Having gained the stance, the belay is transferred to the second man and the leader tackles the second pitch. When he has completed this pitch and is firmly belayed on a stance, the second man brings up the third man to join him above pitch one. When the third man is belayed the second climbs pitch two. At any one time two climbers are belayed while one is actively climbing. The second man's task is unenviable since he is always engaged in looking after the leader, the third man or is climbing himself. He has no opportunity to relax.

Climbing in a rope of three is a safe but lengthy procedure. The quickest way to ascend a rock face is to climb with a partner of similar ability to yourself and to use the technique of leading through. When the leader reaches the stance at the top of the first pitch he belays in the normal way and brings up his partner to join him. However the belay is not transferred to the second man, who now takes over the lead and climbs pitch two. It is a system of alternating the lead pitch by pitch. There is a minimum of rope re-organization and much time is saved.

Most climbs have one pitch that is distinctly harder than the others, this is called the crux pitch. Amusing scenes are often witnessed at the start of a climb with each climber working out, from the guide book, whether leading the first pitch will mean leading the crux pitch later on. Surprisingly perhaps, most climbers like to lead the crux pitch themselves and thus they vie for the privilege. The fairest system is to toss a coin for the first pitch and accept what comes later.

This then is an outline description of the techniques of rope management as used for rock climbing. But before you dash off into the mountains to try it for yourself read the rest of this chapter because it is a technique that must be carried out correctly. You would be safer to climb without any rope at all rather than to use it in a slipshod or dangerous fashion. Safety equipment is improving all the time and the experts are seldom caught out. Compared with the number of active rock climbers, accidents are rare and the few that do happen usually involve inexperienced and over-ambitious climbers.

The rope

The rope is the rock climber's most prized possession. A coil of new, brightly coloured kernmantel rope is an object of beauty as well as being highly versatile and functional.

Nylon or perlon is the material that is universally in use and on no account should you be tempted to use an old hemp rope which you have found in the attic. White cable-laid nylon climbing ropes are still the cheapest on the market but I would advise you to spend a bit more and buy a kernmantel rope. Kernmantel ropes consist of long nylon fibres encased in a tightly woven sheath. The absence of twisted fibres means that the rope runs freely without any tendency to kink. The braided sheaths can now be made with fluorescent dyes for climbing in poor light and they are impregnated with water-resistant chemicals to keep the rope dry and light. Many different patterns and colours are available (*see fig. 1*).

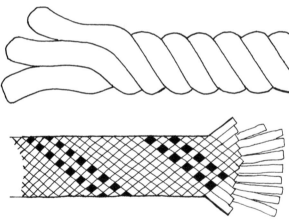

Fig. 1 Cable laid and kernmantel rope

Make sure you buy a rope that is strong enough and long enough. A diameter of 11 millimetres and a length of 40 metres is about right. The British Standard for this weight of rope is BS 3104, No. 4. A typical manufacturer's specification for a climbing rope would be:

Diameter	11 mm.
Weight per metre	76 g.
Breaking load	2750 kg.
Stretch at breaking point	48%
Stretch at 80 kg. load	3.6%

These figures show at a glance the advantages of nylon climbing ropes. They are light, they are exceptionally strong and they stretch under load. The momentum of a falling climber is gradually destroyed by the rope as it stretches and the force is unlikely to exceed the breaking load. The high degree of elasticity means that the climber is less likely to be injured by a sudden jerk, particularly since the second man should also provide some slip or give when the rope becomes taut. On the other hand there is little stretch under low load so a climber using the rope for an abseil does not spring up and down like a yo-yo.

Statistics on the breaking strain of ropes and the tension caused by falling climbers are notoriously misleading and the BMC has a committee whose task it is to compile and interpret the mass of information that is accruing all the time.

One should not become too complacent about the high breaking load of an 11-millimetre nylon rope, for the figures represent ideal conditions. The breaking load can be drastically reduced by certain practices. Nylon melts at a low temperature, well below 500°C and friction, particularly between nylon and nylon, can easily melt a rope. Nylon is damaged by ultra-violet light, chemicals and poor storage. Nylon has limited powers of recovery after absorbing a shock load. If, under load, it is run over a sharp edge or flake of rock it can cut or it can fail because of an inability to undergo its natural extension when jammed in a crack. Here is a list of important safety points regarding nylon climbing rope.

1 Do not misuse the rope. Keep it carefully coiled, without twists or kinks and never use it for towing the car, even if you break down on the motorway. Never tread on the rope.

2 Store the rope in a well-ventilated room away from chemicals and bright sunlight.

3 When climbing try to run the rope over smooth and rounded rocks and not over sharp edges or through cracks.

4 Use recommended knots only. Knots in nylon rope can work loose and they should be checked regularly.

5 Discard the rope at the first sign of serious wear or following several shock loads. In any event a rope should be replaced after two or three years of regular use. Old ropes are ideal for towing cars but not for rock climbing.

6 Never borrow a rope unless you are absolutely sure of its past history and never lend a rope unless you are confident that it will not be ill-treated.

7 Nylon belay slings must never be directly linked to other nylon slings or to the main climbing rope; the friction generated will rapidly melt the rope. Link them through karabiners.

Bear in mind that your safety when climbing depends on the weakest link in the chain of safeguards. It is not sufficient to climb with a brand new 11-millimetre kernmantel rope if your waist band or harness, 'D' ring, karabiner and belay slings are of inferior quality.

The rule is to use, whenever possible, the main climbing rope for belaying since this is likely to be the strongest rope you have with you. Only use belay slings when it is inconvenient or impossible to use the main rope. It may be that the 11-millimetre rope is too thick to pass behind the belay block or there is not enough rope to spare for belaying purposes. If this is the case use the strongest slings you have with you and use them double for extra security. Belay slings made from nylon tape or webbing are extremely practical. They can be flat or hosed and a tape of only 2-millimetre thickness, which can easily be tucked into a thin crack, can have a breaking load of 2700 kilos. When tying up slings of nylon tape you must use the special knot as described later in this chapter.

Carry a selection of slings, at least seven or eight of varying thicknesses and lengths. I always carry one or two slings fitted with a leather sleeve to stop chaffing if the sling has to run over a sharp edge of rock. You will soon discover for yourself, when leading a climb, that feelings of vertigo and exposure vanish when running belays are secured. To run out of slings before the crux is reached is an agonizing experience.

If the main rope runs over a bulge of rock use extra-long running belay slings or fasten two together as this allows the rope to run freely down to the second man without excessive friction (*see fig. 2*). However clever you are at arranging running belays you will find that

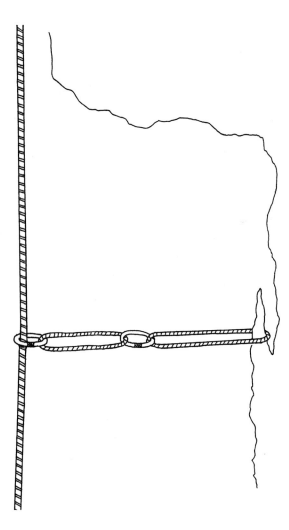

Fig. 2 The use of two slings to prevent friction against the rock

usually they cause friction. I have often found it necessary to pause before a delicate move and pull up enough slack to allow me to move up without rope drag. On long pitches with many overhangs most climbers use two 9-millimetre ropes and clip them alternately into the running belays to reduce friction.

When you have reached the top of your climb you should coil up the rope neatly. If you drag it down or throw it from the top of the cliff it could be easily damaged. Coil it quite loosely, allowing the coils to form naturally. If there are twists or kinks shake them out towards the free end and do not force the rope into shapes which it resists. Finally, bind the coils firmly with a simple whipping (*see fig. 3*).

Fig. 3 Whipping a coiled rope

Knots

Lengthy and involved instruction in knot tying has put many people off the sport of rock climbing. They have my sympathy, for climbing is mainly about airy ascents of rock faces which provide thrills and exhilaration rather than the intricacies of knot tying. However, knots are a small but vital part of the sport and the important knots are soon learned. There are, of course, dozens of different knots for all purposes and eventualities but I propose to concentrate on just a very few. It is much better to be 100 per cent confident of tying the few really essential knots than to have a vague knowledge of a wide variety of weird and wonderful, but complicated, knots.

1 *The fisherman's knot* – A belay loop should be tied with a single or double fisherman's knot (*see fig. 4*), unless the loop is to be made with nylon tape, in which case it is essential that the special non-slip knot for tapes be used (*see fig. 5*).

Fig. 5 A non-slip knot for tape slings

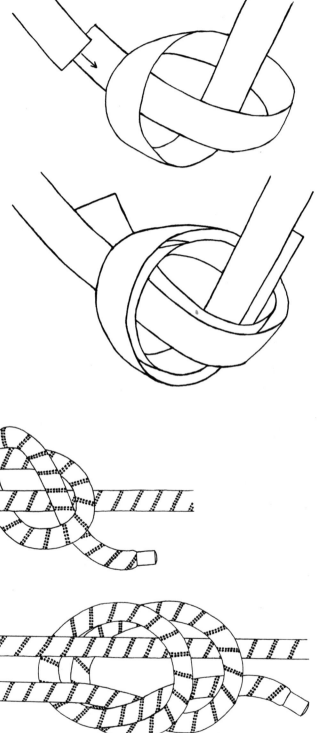

Fig. 4 The single and double fisherman's knot

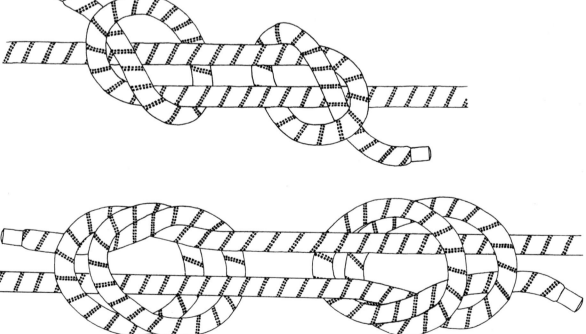

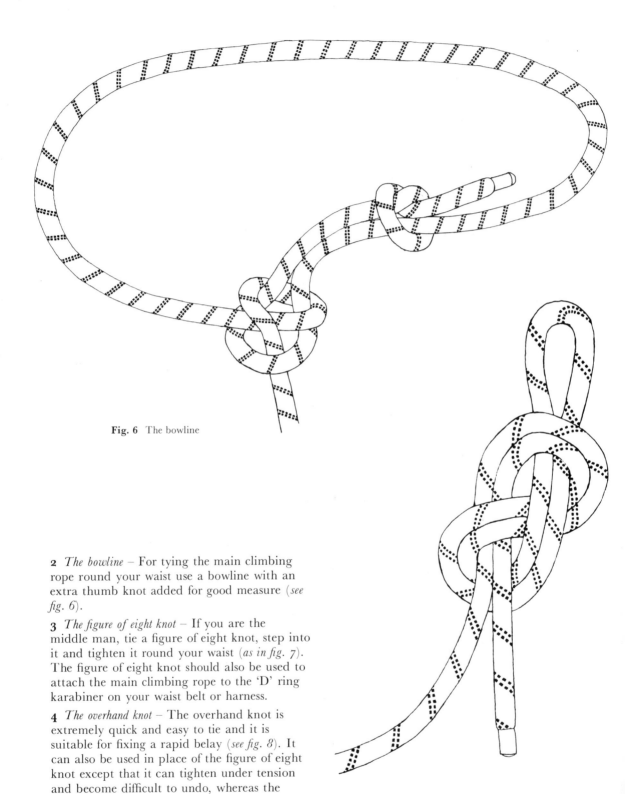

Fig. 6 The bowline

2 *The bowline* – For tying the main climbing rope round your waist use a bowline with an extra thumb knot added for good measure (*see fig. 6*).

3 *The figure of eight knot* – If you are the middle man, tie a figure of eight knot, step into it and tighten it round your waist (*as in fig. 7*). The figure of eight knot should also be used to attach the main climbing rope to the 'D' ring karabiner on your waist belt or harness.

4 *The overhand knot* – The overhand knot is extremely quick and easy to tie and it is suitable for fixing a rapid belay (*see fig. 8*). It can also be used in place of the figure of eight knot except that it can tighten under tension and become difficult to undo, whereas the figure of eight tends not to jam.

Fig. 7 The figure of eight knot

Karabiners

Karabiners or 'krabs' are vital items of the rock climber's equipment. These metal links with sprung gates are used in conjunction with loops, slings, running belays, waist bands, pitons and descendeurs (*see fig. 9*). Remember that nylon must never run against nylon and karabiners must always be used as the intermediate link. Recent advances in technology have meant that very lightweight alloy karabiners, with no loss of strength, are available on the market. Nevertheless the quality of karabiners is governed by the UIAA (Union Internationale des Associations d'Alpinisme) standard, so make sure that any you buy conform to this specification. The standard takes into account the strength of the latch, the pin and the sideways loading of the karabiner as well as its over-all breaking load.

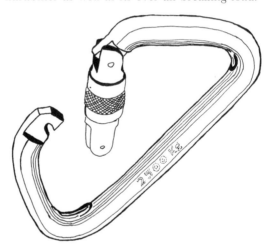

Fig. 9 A screw gate karabiner

Buy a large screw gate karabiner for your waist band. Use it to clip the figure of eight knot on the main climbing rope to the 'D' ring of your belt. It must be large enough to take several thicknesses of 11-millimetre rope for this will be necessary when fixing a belay.

For running belays lighter karabiners will suffice but for complete security they should be fitted with screw gates and the screw should always be tightened. Although the sprung gate of a karabiner closes with a satisfying click, there have been several cases when the gate has opened inadvertently with disastrous results. It is possible for the rope, under tension, to

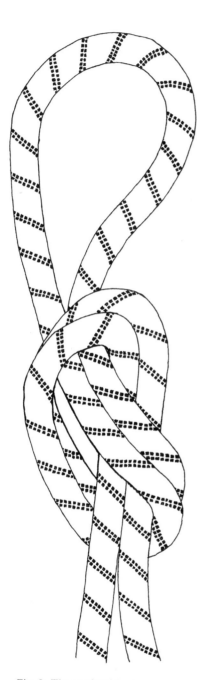

Fig. 8 The overhand knot

ride over the gate and force it open. The gate may be pressed against the rock with the same result. Your anorak could become jammed in the gate preventing proper closure. The twisting action of one karabiner against another or against a piton could open the gate. Using a screw gate karabiner guards against all those dangers.

Practise using karabiners until you can operate them quickly and efficiently with either the left or the right hand. You may be leading up a steep wall and require to fix a running belay; one hand will be needed to keep you in balance and the other must deal with the runner. Karabiners are just as important as the rope for safe rock climbing and they should be carefully tended. Never drop a karabiner for the shock can damage the structure of the metal and weaken it. Mark your karabiners with a coloured piece of sticky tape or a blob of paint, for if you don't you will find they go missing very quickly. A much used karabiner can become a firm favourite and the use of it, with a runner, can inspire confidence on a hard pitch.

Belts and harnesses

If you are using a waist bowline make sure that it is sufficiently tight because if you do have the misfortune to fall, and you find yourself dangling on the rope, the waist loop can ride up to your chest and restrict your breathing. Climbers have been known to lose consciousness quite rapidly by such an occurrence. Experiment for yourself and you will discover that dangling from the rope is an excruciating experience. It is far better to stay on the rock!

The waist loop problem can be solved by using a broad belt of nylon webbing which fastens round the waist with a grip buckle. Since nylon webbing is rather slippery it is vital to tuck the end of the belt back through the fastener to make it absolutely secure (*see fig. 10*). Most climbing belts have sliding 'D' rings for ease of attachment to karabiners.

Even better are the various seat and chest or whole body harnesses which are available from the manufacturers. I use a Whillans' seat

Fig. 10 Fastening a waist belt buckle

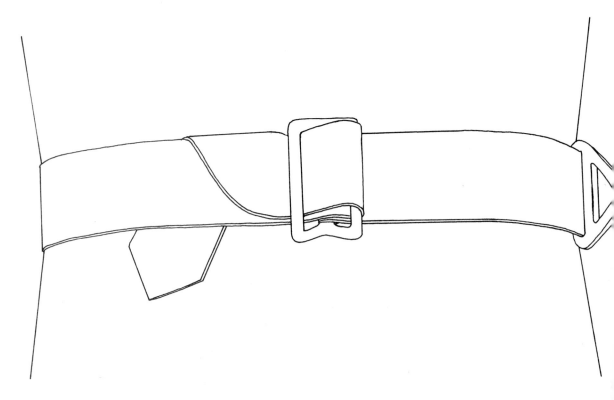

harness because I find the various extra points of attachment for suspending nuts and wedges are most useful. I have never liked chest harnesses, I find them restricting and bothersome, and they nullify the feelings of ease and free movement, the *raison d'être* of the rock climber.

Do not make do with a nylon sling for a waist loop, particularly one which is fastened with a karabiner (*as in fig. 11*). Such an arrangement exerts a three-way pull on the karabiner and since they are not designed for this purpose they could fail under load.

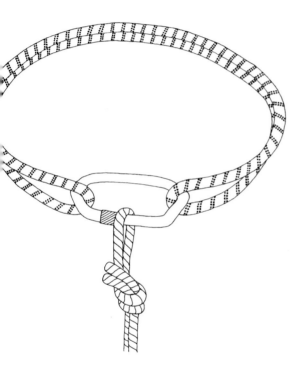

Fig. 11 A three-way pull on a karabiner (not recommended)

Belaying

Good belays are the key to enjoyable rock climbing. A sound belay raises morale and increases confidence, whereas a doubtful belay breeds timidity and indecisiveness.

Belaying with the main climbing rope is extravagant on rope but it is the best method. Pass the rope round the belay block and then pass a bight of it up through your waist band or belt. Pull through at least a metre of rope and tie two half-hitches around all three standing ropes (*see fig. 12*). Make sure that your body is tight up against the belay rope so that you will suffer the minimum jerk if tension comes on to the climbing rope. You might think that it is a simple task for a leader to hold a falling second, who, in theory, should not suffer much drop before being pulled up short. I must emphasize though that it is never easy to hold a falling climber and many complacent leaders have been pulled off their stances by falling seconds. If there is not enough main climbing rope available you must use a belay sling (*see fig. 13*).

Thread belays are amongst the most satisfactory and if natural chockstones are not already in place, artificial nuts or chocks may be inserted in the crack. This technique has developed gradually over the last twenty years and it is now well established. The first innovators carried pockets full of various-sized pebbles which they slotted into cracks, then followed ordinary metal nuts threaded with nylon cord. Nowadays specially designed hexagonal chocks, asymmetrical chocks and wedges are constructed of light but tough alloy and the latest invention is a sprung toggle which, it is claimed, will jam itself safely into even smooth-sided parallel cracks (*see fig. 14*).

My own opinion is that any new device which increases the safety of the climber is an important advance provided that it is removed after the climb without trace. I am totally against the indiscriminate use of pitons on our classic British rock climbs. Artificial climbing, which relies completely on the use of aids such as pitons, rock drills and expansion bolts, should be confined to certain overhanging cliffs where there is no possibility of an ascent by any other method. I would make an exception on certain exposed climbs using tiny stances where there is no other safe way of fixing a belay.

In the Alps and Himalayas it is essential to carry a hammer and a few pitons because the hazards and difficulties are so much greater than on British hills. An unexpectedly wet or iced pitch may require a piton for direct aid or to speed up an ascent in the face of threatening weather. A quick retreat may be a life-saving

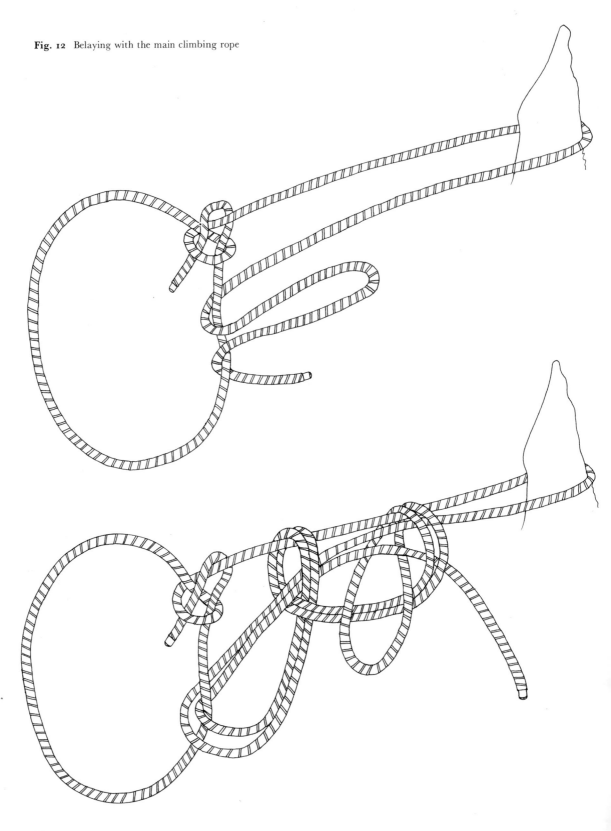

Fig. 12 Belaying with the main climbing rope

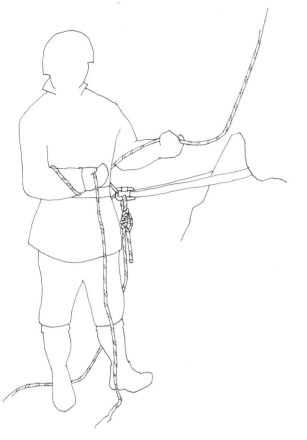

Fig. 13 Belaying with a sling

Fig. 14 Artificial nuts and chocks

operation and abseils from pitons may be the only way down. But it is unforgivable to bang in pitons on Tryfan or Scafell whenever the going gets tough. It is still in the best traditions of British rock climbing to use pitons sparingly.

There has always been lively debate in British mountaineering circles about the extent to which artificial aids should be used. As early as 1892 eyebrows were raised by a report that J.N. Collie, on the first ascent of the now classic Moss Ghyll climb on Scafell, had nicked a tiny foothold on a sloping slab with his ice axe to facilitate the exit from a difficult chimney. This tiny nick, known as the Collie Step, is there to this day.

In 1936 a team of crack German climbers, including the redoubtable Teufel, were invited to Britain to climb on the best of British rock in Snowdonia. They succeeded in putting up a new route called Munich climb on the east face of Tryfan but they used three pitons in the process. The climbing establishment was up in arms and forthwith a powerful British team, led by Wilfrid Noyce, removed the pitons and repeated the climb free of aid. The honour of British climbing was restored.

A good belay can lull a climber into a false

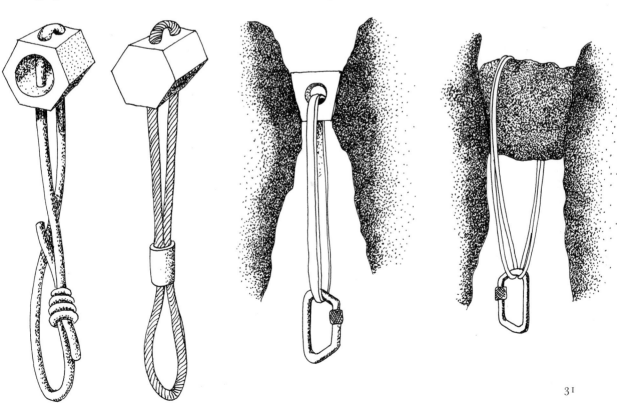

7 Placing a running belay on Jasper climb. (Photograph by R. Keates)

sense of security and I shall finish this section with two important pleas.

1 When the second man arrives on the leader's stance, clip the second's waist band into the belay karabiner before the leader undoes his own belay prior to continuing the climb. In this way both climbers are secure the whole time.

2 Take very special care at the top of the climb. Don't untie from the rope until you are sure that all difficulties have been passed. Walk well back from the edge of the cliff before sorting out the slings and coiling the rope. It has been known for climbers to trip over the rope at the top of a climb and plunge down over the edge of the cliff.

Communications

On simple rock climbs with short pitches it is very easy to see exactly what is going on. The second man can watch the leader climb the pitch, reach the stance, belay himself and begin to take in the slack. He can then untie his belay and start climbing. Imagine, however, a long pitch climbed on a windy day when the leader soon climbs up out of sight of the second man and carries on upwards until the rope between them becomes taut. Does the second man know that the leader is belayed and that he is expected to climb up to him? Does the leader know if he has run out of rope?

Very dangerous situations can arise unless all the climbers on a rope know exactly what is happening at all times. Even if the climbers are in each other's sight they must always use the universally understood phraseology of the rock climber.

Leader: 'Runner on'. When a running belay is fixed. The second now knows that he must keep a minimum of slack rope between himself and the leader and that any sudden tension on the rope will be upwards.

Leader: 'I'm there'. To inform the second that he has reached the stance.

Leader: 'Taking in'. To inform the second that he is pulling in the slack rope.

Second: 'That's me'. To inform the leader that all the slack has now been pulled up.

Leader: 'Come on up'. To tell the second that all is ready for him to start climbing.

Second: 'Climbing'.

Second: 'Slack'. A request to the leader to let down a short length of slack.

Second: 'Take in'. A request to the leader to pull up accumulated slack.

Second: 'Tight rope!' A desperate plea to the leader for direct assistance from the rope.

If the climbers are out of earshot a simple system of tugs on the rope should be devised and thoroughly understood. I use a system of three sharp tugs from the leader to inform the second that all is ready for him, the second, to start climbing. Likewise three tugs from the second tells the leader that there is still some slack to be taken in.

If the leader's recurrent nightmare is a long lead with insufficient running belays, the second's nightmare is following up a hard pitch with great loops of slack rope between himself and the leader, belayed above.

Arresting a fall

Let us suppose that you are belayed on a ledge 100 feet up a rock face and your second, half-way up the first pitch, has suddenly cried out, 'Tight rope'. You have only a few seconds to prepare yourself to take the strain of an 80-kilo weight falling several feet.

Move towards the edge of the ledge until you are really tight up against your belay. Seek any jutting-out rocks or cracks against which you can brace your feet. Bend your knees so that your thigh muscles will take most of the strain.

Very quickly take in any existing slack rope between yourself and the second, even a few inches of slack contribute towards an appalling jerk when the strain comes. The climbing rope which passes round your body at waist level should be pulled in towards the centre of your waist to maximize the friction that is available. The rope on the side away from the climber should pass once round your forearm before being firmly gripped in gloved hands to guard against rope burns (*as in fig. 15*). When the strain comes, allow the rope to slip slightly through your gloved hands until the momentum of the falling body is absorbed. Next, lower the climber very slowly down the face until he can regain purchase on the rock at a lower level.

Fig. 15 The correct position for arresting a fall

If the climber decides not to make another attempt on the pitch, insist that he climbs back down to the ground. This will be good for his confidence and will save further unnecessary strain on the rope. You will be left unattended on the stance and you may have to descend on two abseils unless you have enough rope to climb back down protected by your second via a runner fixed at the belay stance. The same drill for arresting a fall applies to the second man holding his leader except that the strain on the equipment and on the second is likely to be that much more severe and, assuming a running belay is in place, the pull will be upwards.

I have only once fallen when leading a climb and that was on the slightly overhanging Mur y Niwl (Wall of the Mists) face of Craig-Yr-Ysfa in north Wales. I was attempting the second ascent of a climb called Agrippa and was about 50 feet above the screes and near the end of the first pitch. I reached up and found a rusty piton inserted in a crack; it felt sound and I pulled up on it but when the pull was outwards rather than downwards it popped out and I catapulted backwards into space. Luckily my only runner, at 40 feet, held and I came to rest head downwards above the screes with my second, Nigel Rogers, who had not belayed to the rock, swinging beside me. I was unhurt but the experience was traumatic and it curbed my desire to climb hard routes for several years.

Abseils

I am often amazed to see parties of school children indulging in the practice of abseiling as a sport to provide a diversion on a Saturday afternoon. An abseil or rappel is a method used for emergency descents of rock faces based on sliding down a fixed rope. It is a technique that should be learned and practised but not indulged in, because it is fraught with danger; several well-known climbers have died in abseiling accidents and it imposes considerable strain on the equipment. Nevertheless it is important to be able to fix up an abseil rope quickly and efficiently and it is an essential part of a mountaineer's knowledge and skill.

In the Alps and Himalayas abseiling can be the only safe way down from a mountain and after a long ascent when you are desperately tired, hungry and numb with cold the arranging of abseils must be second nature.

Abseils may be necessary to reach the start of sea cliff climbs when the tide does not allow an approach from below. They may be necessary in order to recce a hard move by descending the rock face from above or to reclaim a tightly jammed nut, wedge or sling. The principle of the abseil is simple. The main climbing rope is placed around a convenient block, spike, or chockstone, or it is passed through a rope loop which is itself secured to a jammed nut or wedge or to a piton. The climbers then descend the doubled rope until they reach a convenient ledge or, if the rope is long enough, the bottom of the cliff. By pulling hard on one end, the rope is retrieved and the process is repeated as required. The advantage of climbing on doubled 9-millimetre rope, rather than on a single 11-millimetre rope, is that twice the distance can be descended in a single abseil.

Various techniques have been developed for descending the doubled rope but I intend to describe only three of them. Each has its own particular merit.

1 *The traditional method (see fig. 16).* This method needs the minimum of equipment but it can be extremely uncomfortable unless a jersey, anorak and thick cord breeches are worn. A lot of friction is generated by the rope and there is no chance of a runaway descent. The rate of abseil is determined by the grip of the right hand round the trailing rope.

2 *The sling seat (see fig. 17).* The climber sits in a simple figure of eight seat constructed from a nylon sling and held in place by a screw gate karabiner. The rope runs through the karabiner and no longer passes under the thigh. It is an improvement on the traditional method but shoulder and back scuffing can still occur.

3 *Using the descendeur.* The descendeur is a friction brake device. There are several models on the market but I shall describe only one of them, the simplest. Once again simplicity is all important, for mistakes in operating descendeurs have occurred. The figure of eight descendeur is illustrated in fig. 18. It is made of thick alloy so that any heat generated by

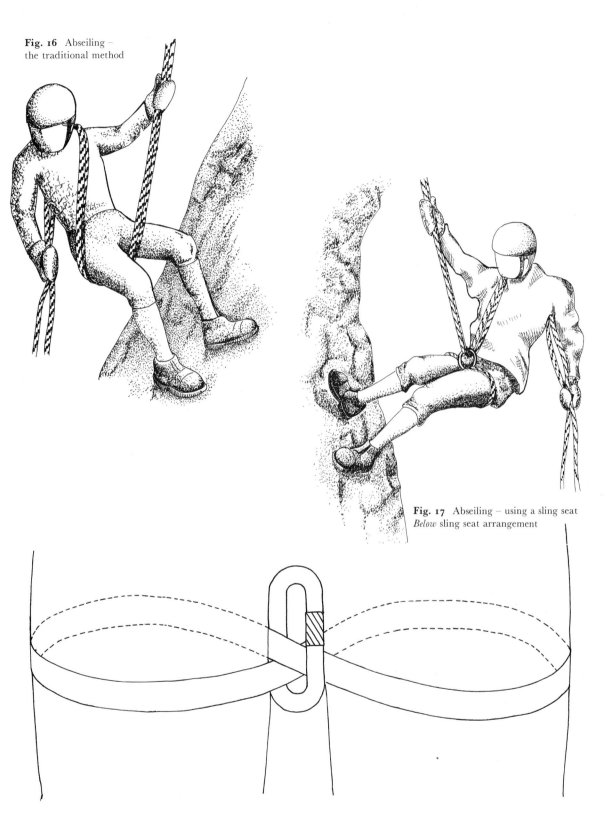

Fig. 16 Abseiling –
the traditional method

Fig. 17 Abseiling – using a sling seat
Below sling seat arrangement

35

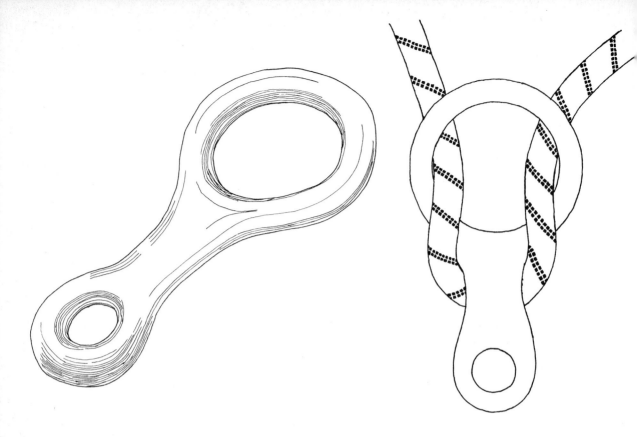

Fig. 18 The figure of eight descendeur

friction is quickly dissipated. On a very long abseil it is advisable to keep moving to guard against the (unlikely) event of the descendeur heating up sufficiently to melt the rope.

The descendeur is clipped into the waist band 'D' ring using a karabiner; it provides ample friction so the rope need not be passed round the back and shoulders. The friction, and hence the speed of descent, is easily controlled by altering the exit angle of the trailing rope.

When abseiling it is best to lower yourself until your body makes an angle of about 70° with the cliff face and to place the soles of your boots flat against the rock. In this way you will minimize any tendency to twist. As you descend, look down at regular intervals to check that the rope is hanging free and that both ends are together. If one end is longer than the other and you transfer to a single rope disaster will follow immediately.

Before you start a descent by abseil check the anchor point of the rope to ensure both that it is sound and that the rope runs freely. Most climbers I know have suffered maddening delays and frustration caused by jammed abseil ropes. A few years ago I was climbing in the Cuillin hills of Skye with a party of six or seven boys. We all climbed the famous Inaccessible Pinnacle, lunched on top, and abseiled the 50 or 60 feet back to the ground. When we came to pull down the abseil rope we discovered that it was firmly jammed. The entire party was heaving on one end of the rope when to our horror an enormous boulder, the anchor point, became dislodged and it crashed on to the screes beside us before breaking into a thousand pieces and rumbling down the gully into Coire Lagan. The rope was free but at a high cost to our nervous systems.

I strongly advise any party abseiling down a cliff to use a safety rope, particularly if they are novices or children. Of course the last man down cannot enjoy the protection of a safety rope but by then the rope and the anchor point will have been thoroughly tested.

One final point. Never run the main climbing rope directly through a nylon belay loop. Use either a strong hemp or manilla loop, or else sacrifice a karabiner.

8 The abseil. (Photograph by R. Karl)

Guide books and choice of route

Unless you are lucky enough, on your mountaineering expeditions, to find a new and undiscovered rock face you will have to be content with repeating routes which have previously been climbed. There is something particularly satisfying about pioneering a new route, whether it is on a new or existing crag. The spirit of true exploration runs deep in many of us. But you will need to gain much experience first, because the ascent of a new route involves extra and often unforeseen difficulties. A new route will need gardening, that is the clearing away of loose rock, moss and tussocks of grass; the leader will need extra confidence and skill to move around blind corners and up narrow cracks not knowing what lies ahead.

However, it is valuable to learn from the experiences of others and most cliffs have their own guide books which provide all sorts of information on the various climbs. These guide books are often published by climbing clubs both for the benefit of their members and other climbers, and to raise money for club funds. Here are some of the details which a well-written climbing guide should provide.

1 General background information about the crag; the height, the type of rock and the best way of approach. Local accommodation.

2 A historical survey of the development of the crag as a climbing ground.

3 An accurate diagram of the rock face showing clearly the principal features and climbs.

4 A complete list of the climbs giving their grades and the number and length of each of the pitches.

5 A comment on each climb giving an assessment of the climb's character, exposure and merit. Some guide books assess quality by a star rating system while others cover several crags and give only details of 'recommended' climbs. This is useful if you can pay only a fleeting visit to a particular area and want to tackle the best climbs.

In the second half of the nineteenth century mountaineers started to turn their attention to rock faces. Groups of climbers would meet every weekend at the Wastdale Head Hotel in Lakeland and at Pen-y-Pass in Snowdonia and before long some of our great clubs were founded. These were the Scottish Mountaineering Club in 1889, the Climbers Club in 1898 and the Fell and Rock Climbing Club in 1906.

These early climbers concentrated on the natural lines of weakness on a rock face, the arêtes, the chimneys, the cracks and the buttresses. Such climbs have become 'classic' and are nearly always amongst the best, though not usually the hardest, on the cliff. The greatest classic of the Lake District is, without doubt, Central Buttress route on Scafell. This bold climb, 470-feet long, takes an almost direct line up the cleanest sweep of rock in England. It was first climbed in 1914 by Herford, Sansom and Holland and, remarkably, its grade of Hard Very Severe has withstood the test of time. Central Buttress is a must for the experienced rock climber and even with modern safety equipment it is a serious undertaking.

It is the character of a rock climb, rather than the passage of time since its first ascent, that qualifies it to reach 'classic' status. Ever since climbers started to explore north Wales the natural line of Cenotaph Corner has endowed it with exceptional quality. Cenotaph Corner plunges down the Dinas Y Gromlech cliff in the Llanberis Pass. Like an open book it splits two smooth rock faces by a narrow overhanging crack, fully 120-feet long with no intermediate stances. It was finally climbed in 1952 by Joe Brown and immediately it became a 'classic'. Aptly named, it lies adjacent to Cemetery Gates, Ivy Sepulchre and Sexton's Route.

The grading of climbs can be rather arbitrary. The method adopted depends on the country, the club responsible for the guide book and the editor. In the first instance the naming of a new climb and the allocating of a grade is the privilege of the climber who made the first ascent. In Britain the grades are:

1 Easy
2 Moderate
3 Difficult
4 Very Difficult
5 Severe
6 Very Severe
7 Extremely Severe

On the continent of Europe the corresponding grades are I to VI and this system is creeping into British guide books, particularly in Scotland. The grades refer to good weather and dry rock and they can be drastically altered by wet or freezing conditions. The higher categories of grades are often sub-divided to give narrower limits, thus a Severe climb could be described as Mild Severe or Hard Severe. Artificial climbs have their own grades of severity, A1, A2 and A3. Thus it is that a climb classified as Extremely Severe and A3 would, in addition to being a most exacting rock climb, require much technical expertise.

The subject of grading always provokes heated discussion amongst climbers both during and after the climb. A climber on form on a warm summer's day may remark on the comparative ease with which he surmounted the crux and he may think the pitch overgraded. More common though, are remarks like – 'That move was desperate. Very Difficult, never! More like Hard Severe!'

Certain cliffs have built up their own reputations. Most of my early rock climbing was performed on limestone, Northumbrian Whinsill and the rhyolitic lavas of north Wales, and as a result, when I visited the Peak District, I found the climbing on rounded weathered gritstone to be very much harder.

The nearest rock climbing to London is at Harrison's Rocks near Tunbridge Wells. The rock is sandstone and the holds are poor. Very special techniques are required and there are exceptional exponents in the art of climbing at Harrison's. These experts tend to abhor Welsh rock, they do not feel at home and their special skills cannot be applied.

Let us suppose that you have arrived at the rock face with your climbing partner and you are flicking through the guide book trying to choose a suitable route for your first ever rock climb. Confine your attention to climbs of Difficult standard, for an Easy or Moderate route is little more than a scramble and may prove to be an anti-climax. Try to find a climb with short but varied pitches. The short pitches will give you practice in rope management and the variety will give you a taste of the different

9 Joe Brown on a new route on Anglesey. (Photograph by K. Wilson)

problems facing the rock climber: slabs, walls, cracks, chimneys, mantle shelves, laybacks, delicate moves and strenuous pull-ups.

Don't attempt to move on to hard climbs before you have sampled the best of the easier climbs. If you find you are managing to get up Difficult and Very Difficult quickly, and without fuss, make sure that you are climbing economically and in balance. Are you heaving and thrutching? (a strenuous upwards struggling movement). Are you using your knees? If so, you are not ready to move onto higher grades. The most important question to ask yourself is 'Am I enjoying my rock climbing?' If the answer is positive and you are happy and confident on the medium-graded climbs, be content and climb some more in this bracket. Every extra climb you complete is adding breadth to your experience. Rock climbers need to serve a sound apprenticeship.

Looking back over many years of rock climbing, some of my happiest memories are of carefree days spent on easy routes. A February day spent on the Terrace Wall of Tryfan when the sun was strong enough to warm the rocks, and smoke from our climbing hut, Helyg in the Ogwen Valley, rose straight up into a clear blue sky. These are romantic memories but I make no excuses for them. Most of us mountaineers are, at heart, romantics and we are fortunate to be able to combine deep emotions with our chosen sport.

Other happy memories are of long days spent on challenging routes. Days when I was keyed up and tense with concentration yet, at the end, supremely satisfied by the day's achievement and revelling in the slow process of relaxation of body and mind.

Rock climbing is becoming more competitive; climbers are taking up the sport at a much younger age and are going straight on to hard rock without the experience of a hill walking and general mountaineering background. It is tough at the top and many of the hard men are motivated by competition – if you don't succeed on the overhang this weekend someone else will succeed next weekend. Standards are shooting up and it is easy to be caught in the competitive spiral, but remember that the

10 Continuation Wall – the best of Welsh rock. (Photograph by K. Leech)

climbs which satisfied the aspirations of previous generations are still there, just as good as ever, and probably a lot better than many of the modern extremes.

A good insight into the relaxed early days of rock climbing is provided by the account of the first ascent of a delightful climb, of Mild Very Severe standard on the east face of Tryfan, called Belle Vue Bastion. It was so named because the ascent, in 1927, was made with a large audience watching and to the accompaniment of a wind-up gramophone on the ledge below. Leisured days indeed.

Rock climbing techniques

Really good rock climbers, like fast bowlers and rugby flyhalfs, are born, not made. I have introduced many young people to rock climbing and those with natural ability have needed no help from me whatsoever apart from instruction in safety techniques. These are the lucky few; most of us benefit from being shown the correct way to climb a rock face and climbing schools cater for this need. A week's course at a climbing school will start you off along the right lines and should mean that you will avoid the dismay and frustration of becoming stuck on a hard move, or the indignity of scrabbling with knees and elbows up a smooth slab.

Before I describe the different problems which may confront you on a rock climb let me list some of the basic principles of elegant and economical climbing.

1 As far as possible let your feet or toes support the weight of your body. Your arms are much weaker than your legs and they have limited strength which should be preserved for the occasions when they really have to be used. Overhangs, laybacks and hand traverses rely almost entirely on arm strength.

2 Stand well away from the rock so that your centre of gravity is over your feet. In this way you minimize the need for friction to keep your boots on the rock. It is natural, at first, to want to hug the rock but this increases the likelihood of a slip. Apart from the considerations of friction it is very difficult to see the rocks above your head and to work out your next move if you are too close.

3 At all times try to find more than two sound points of attachment to the rock. Never completely rely on a single hold because boots can slip and flakes of rock can fracture. A safe climber always has a second line of defence in case of a sudden emergency.

4 If you move up a rock face without having first worked out the sequence of holds that you are going to use, you will probably spend time in an unbalanced position and rapidly become exhausted. Work out a plan of attack and then move swiftly and surely.

5 Try to avoid kneeling on holds. It is almost always possible to make a high step and thus save bruising the knees; besides which it is often extremely hard to get up again into a standing position.

6 Always listen to your instincts. If you feel your strength beginning to fade, find a resting place and pause until you feel confident of continuing. If you rush on up, hoping for the best, you are likely to end up dangling on the rope and feeling humiliated. If in doubt, go back down. I have often retreated on a climb and although I have felt disappointed for a short time afterwards, I have soon felt thankful at the decision. Mountaineering is too sweet a pastime to take unnecessary risks with the chance of ending it all. There will always be another day and another chance of completing the route.

Easy climbs have plenty of obvious holds and usually one may use a number of combinations of them to make the ascent. Hard climbs have very few holds, they are not always obvious and they are much smaller. You will soon learn how to use the available holds to their best advantage, perhaps a side pull here, a bridging move there or a low pressure hold to keep you in balance. Any person with an average physique should be able to tackle climbs of up to Severe standard because all the holds will be there. The difficulty is to work out how to use the holds and this cannot always be done straight away. If the move you are about to make seems disproportionately hard for the grade of climb you are on, step down, resurvey the rock and try to find an extra hold or a different combination of holds. Don't give up; the more you put into a climb the greater the sense of satisfaction when it has been conquered.

11 Good technique on Milestone Buttress, Tryfan. The climber, Sean Williams, is keeping well away from the rock. (Photograph by John Cleare)

For your first climb you would do well to avoid gullies. Although gullies were explored before anything else by the early.climbers they are often wet, greasy and loose. Find a rock face or an outcrop that is open to the elements – these faces dry quickly and give you the unique sense of exposure and the panoramic views which are so appealing to the mountaineer. If, when you finish your climb, you can walk on up and take in a mountain summit, so much the better. You will have enjoyed a proper mountaineering day.

Slabs

Slabs are sweeps of rock set at an angle of anything between 45° and 65°. They often have cracks or incut holds but you will find that friction holds are the most common.

Make sure you are wearing the correct footwear to provide the best friction. Vibram-soled boots, Kletterschuhe, EBs or a pair of old gym shoes are all suitable. Remember to keep well away from the rock to minimize the need for friction. This is extremely important for slab climbing because your feet or toes are providing the only safe anchor points on the rock. Hand holds are often sloping and inadequate except to help in maintaining balance. Keep your hands as low down as possible because in this way the correct posture is most easily assumed.

You will find that any extra rugosities, concavities, pockets or bulges on the surface of the rock make extremely useful holds. Crystalline rock will support a climber, wearing the correct footwear, at a remarkably high angle but, as a general rule, you should never simply place your foot on a sloping rock and hope for the best – it might slip. In wet weather, slabs can become treacherous and are best left alone. If you are caught by a sudden shower you will find that socks stretched over your boots, or just stockinged feet, will provide better friction than rubber.

12 Correct position for slab climbing. (Photograph by K. Wilson)

The application of the correct technique is of paramount importance for slab climbing and it is a good idea to select a slab as your first ever rock climb. Once the technique has been learned it can be applied to steeper and more demanding climbs such as walls.

In north Wales the 400-foot Idwal Slabs provide a selection of easy angled but superb slab climbs ranging in standard from Moderate to Severe. Generations of climbers have started their climbing careers here, in Cwm Idwal, in this most tranquil of settings. Below the screes is the expanse of Llyn Idwal, while at the head of the Cwm the rock buttresses are split by the deep defile of the Devil's Kitchen and across the Ogwen Valley rises the huge bulk of the Carneddau range. The Ordinary Route is a groove, packed with good holds, which runs up the centre of the slabs while on each side rise three slab climbs of high quality, Faith, Hope and Charity. Hugging the left-hand edge of the slabs is the delicate Tennis Shoe climb, so named because rubber soled tennis shoes, rather than nailed boots, were worn for the first ascent in 1919.

In the Lake District an amusing little slab climb is found on Lower Scout Crag in Langdale. This one pitch climb ascends well-worn slabs at an easy angle until near the top they steepen to a short wall. The wall is easily surmounted by a determined heave over a jammed chockstone which rocks outwards at the crucial moment. It is quite sound but the few inches of movement are enough to give an unsuspecting climber a leaping heart.

Recommended slab climbs

Grooved Arete (850 feet). Very Difficult on the east face of Tryfan. This superb climb contains the classic Knight's Slab. Poised above a vertical face, the climber moves up and then across this slab of clean rock as in the Knight's move on the chess board.

Great Slab (620 feet). Very Severe on Clogwyn Du'r Arddu, north Wales. This is one of the longest and most exposed continuous slab climbs in the country.

Botterill's Slab (140 feet). Very Severe on Scafell. A magnificently clean slab of rock ascending the central section of Scafell West Buttress.

13 The Knight's Move on Grooved Arete, Tryfan. A classic slab pitch. (Photograph by K. Wilson)

The Nose Direct (245 feet). Very Severe on Dinas Mot, north Wales. A fine delicate climb up the centre of the face.

Amphitheatre Buttress (970 feet). Difficult on Craig Yr Ysfa, north Wales. This is a long mountaineering route with some excellent slab pitches. It is exposed and dramatic in places but the standard is not too hard.

Walls

If a slab is tilted towards the vertical it becomes a wall and the rock climber needs to use his hands and arms to preserve his balance. His weight should still be taken on his toes but if the footholds are poor he will need his arms to contribute to the maintenance of his position

14 J. Hoskins doing a hand traverse on Nose Direct, Dinas Mot, Snowdonia. (Photograph by K. Wilson)

15 Little Chamonix climb. Shepherd's Crag, Lakeland. (Photograph by C. Hall)

on the rock. The best kind of hand hold is the one in which the climber can get his hand right round in a firm grip, and is called a 'jug handle'. However, opportunities for jug handles are usually in short supply and he must make do with anything that is available, such as pressure holds, pinch holds, side holds, undercut holds, pockets, cracks and friction holds on sloping ledges. All these can provide enough purchase for the climber to keep on his foot holds, although they might not suffice to bear all his weight if his feet came off.

If holds are not to be found, a finger, hand or fist jam in a crack might be possible. With practice you should find that a hand jam is nearly as good as a jug handle and it is feasible for a single hand jam to bear the entire weight

of a climber for a short time. Don't wear a wrist watch when hand jamming and be prepared for the back of your hand to get scratched by rock crystals – a small price to pay for the successful completion of a major climb. The sure signs of a climber having spent the winter training on gritstone outcrops, in preparation for serious routes in the summer, are scarred backs to his hands. Gritstone, with its rounded and weathered cracks, lends itself particularly well to hand jamming techniques.

Insert your hand into the crack and then force your thumb down towards the palm, jamming it between the rough sides of the crack. For a wider crack insert your fist and pull it down until the crack narrows. Now tightly clench the fist, which will expand, jam in the crack, and

16 A hand jam on Peapod route. (Photograph by R. Keates)

Fig. 19 Hand and fist jams

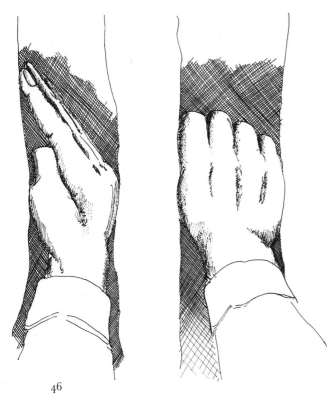

can be used as a makeshift hold (*see fig. 19*).

On a long wall pitch where there are no resting places, the leader's position is most precarious. He will be fully conscious of the exposure and the need to arrange as many running belays as possible. Finding a suitable crack for a jammed nut may not be easy and while he selects the correct nut and sling combination or threads a sling around a chockstone, he will be hanging on by one hand only. He must be quick and adept at placing runners and clipping karabiners into the main climbing rope, so there is no room for tangles or fumbles. Once a secure runner has been placed, a tired leader may use it to rest on. He can hook an elbow through the sling and flex his fingers and hands until his bulging wrists have recovered, and his strength has returned.

Wall climbing calls for speed, balance and confidence. For me it is the purest and most satisfying type of rock climbing.

Recommended wall climbs
Main Wall on Cyrn Las (460 feet). Severe. Llanberis Pass, north Wales. This magnificent route, high above the valley, has many exposed pitches as it ascends the left edge of the Central Buttress. Save this climb until you are more experienced, for safe belays can be difficult to arrange.

Avalanche Route (870 feet). Very Difficult. Lliwedd on Snowdon Massif. This classic route on the east buttress has many delightful pitches including the famous 100-foot red wall pitch.

Troutdale Pinnacle (350 feet). Severe. Borrowdale. A fine exposed route which combines walls, grooves and slabs. The final wall pitch is poised 300 feet above the cliff base and it provides an enthralling finish to this superb climb.

The Devil's Kitchen (100 feet). Very Difficult. Cwm Idwal, north Wales. The final 80-foot pitch ascends the steep left wall of the innermost recess of the Devil's Kitchen. Dark and dripping but with good holds, it leads to the daylight above. One of the great Welsh classics in a unique situation.

Chimneys

For anyone with a tendency to suffer from vertigo, chimneys provide ideal training climbs.

Enclosed on two or three sides by rock walls, one has a big choice of holds and it is often quite possible to use bridging techniques alone, dispense with actual holds, and rely solely on friction grips.

Let us suppose that one wall of the chimney is smooth and holdless, while the other has some ledges and indentations. Press your back firmly against the smooth wall and brace your feet against the opposite wall, placing them, if possible, on the holds. Depending on the width of the chimney, your feet may be almost on a level with your waist. You will be surprised at how safe you feel. Even the tiniest of footholds can be used because your strong thigh muscles will be pushing your boots against them very firmly. Now you must begin the process of backing up the chimney. Raise one foot to a higher level and then by pushing below you with the palms of your hands shift your back up the wall. It is an exhausting way of ascent but remarkably secure, since you are wedged across the cleft (*see fig. 20*).

Fig. 21 Bridging up a chimney

If there are holds on each side of the chimney you can use the technique of bridging. Stand astride the chimney looking inwards or outwards as the most comfortable choice indicates. Move up the chimney from hold to hold, low pressure holds for the hands being the most useful; this is a less tiring method than backing up a chimney (*see fig. 21*).

Narrow chimneys are amongst the most desperately exhausting problems met with on a rock climb. Backing up and bridging are both impossible and you are left with a half-wriggling and half-thrutching movement upwards as your only option. Elbow and knee jams can sometimes provide a breathing space.

Monolith Crack on the Gribin Facet in north Wales is one of the best known narrow chimneys. A man of average build needs to strip down to his vest to get into the crack and then the thrutching starts. I once climbed Monolith Crack with a friend who became stuck in the narrowest section, became exhausted, took a deep breath and cracked a rib!

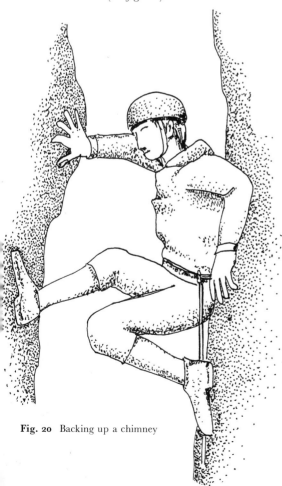

Fig. 20 Backing up a chimney

17 J. Adams on St Bees Chimney. (Photograph by C. Read)

Bridging techniques can sometimes be used to great advantage on climbs that are not true chimneys. On many occasions when climbing steep grooves, walls and corners, the holds have been scarce and my strength has begun to ebb. But by pushing out a foot onto a rock situated behind or to one side of me, thereby providing extra lateral pressure, I have been able to keep in balance.

A 'sentry box' is a short shallow chimney which is blocked off at the top by an overhang. It is often more of an angled corner than a true chimney and if the side walls slope outwards a sentry box can be tricky to climb.

Recommended chimney climbs
Moss Ghyll (430 feet). Very Difficult. Scafell. A classic climb involving no less than five chimney pitches.
New West Climb (290 feet). Difficult. Pillar Rock. Another superb classic climb with several chimney pitches.
Milestone Ordinary (230 feet). Difficult. Tryfan, north Wales. A magnificently varied climb which has several easy and well protected chimney pitches.
Shadbolt's Climb (100 feet). Difficult. Bhasteir Tooth on Cuillin of Skye. This exciting chimney climb leads to a rock tunnel which emerges onto the very summit of the tooth.

Cracks

Close inspection of cracks usually reveals a number of holds. These may be jammed chockstones, side holds deep inside the crack or nicks and ledges on the outside. Completely holdless cracks have to be climbed by jamming techniques as described earlier in this chapter. If the crack is wide enough a shoulder may be inserted and jammed to relieve tired arms and fingers. Twin cracks can sometimes be climbed by placing a hand and foot in each and using a bridging action.

If the walls of a crack are smooth and holdless but are set at an angle to each other like the pages of a half-opened book, the notorious layback method must be used (*see fig. 22*). The hands grip the edge of the crack while the feet

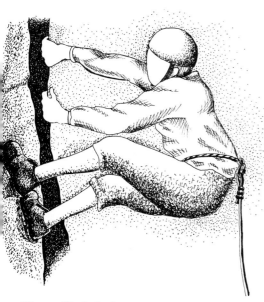

Fig. 22 The layback

are tightly pressed against the smooth opposing wall. The feet should be flat to get maximum friction and they should be placed as high up the wall as possible so that the two forces are directly in opposition. The strain on the hands, arms and shoulders is formidable but a fit climber can pull hard enough for his feet to stay firm and by moving his hands and then his feet, he can progress up the crack.

Don't be tempted to adopt too upright a position while laybacking for, although it eases the strain on the forearms, the angle at which the sideways force is applied to the feet is wrong and the feet could slip. If your feet do slip while you are laybacking there is no way in which you can prevent a fall.

A true layback is an advanced technique and is usually reserved for highly graded climbs but the principle applies to many awkward moves. Side holds, as used in laybacking, can be very valuable if the feet can be braced against a rock to provide an opposing force.

The most famous layback crack of all is the Flake Crack on Central Buttress, Scafell. The crux is surmounted by a short overhanging layback. The move is extremely strenuous and many and legendary are the epics which have been recounted about the Flake Crack. It is probably the most famous single move in British rock climbing. When I came to climb

this crack I was extremely nervous and adrenalin was coursing through my veins at such a rate that I completed the move before I had time to consider whether I was tired or not. My main trouble was nervous tremble.

Recommended routes involving cracks
Amen Corner (15 feet). Severe. A short and slightly overhanging crack which can be combined with either 'B' Route or Bracket and Slab Route on Gimmer Crag in the Lake District.

Little Sepulchre (100 feet). Very Severe. On Drws Gwynt, north Wales. A perfect layback crack set at a reasonable angle.

The Direct Route (300 feet). Severe. On Glyder Fach, north Wales. This is a continuously interesting and varied climb with chimneys, slabs, a hand traverse and several strenuous cracks.

18 Amen Corner. A classic layback crack on Gimmer Crag in Lakeland.

Mantleshelves

Narrow ledges of rock with no other holds above or below must be climbed by mantleshelf moves. Grip the ledge with both hands and pull up until your arms are straight with your shoulders above the ledge and your palms flat on the ledge. Now raise one foot and place it on the ledge (don't use a knee) and then push up on this leg until you are in a standing position (*as in fig. 23*). The rock above the ledge is trying to push you outwards, out of balance, as you make the mantleshelf move, but you can easily practise this at home using a wall or a strong shelf.

Fig. 23 The mantleshelf

One of the most magnificent and exposed climbs in north Wales is the Mur-y-Niwl wall on Craig Yr Ysfa. The crux pitch of the climb involves a traverse out across an overhanging wall using small holds which finally peter out. The climber must then perform a reverse mantleshelf from the final ledge, placing his hands on the ledge and lowering his body down the overhanging wall until his feet reach small holds below. The traverse is then continued at a lower level.

19 The reverse mantleshelf. Mur-y-Niwl, north Wales. (Photograph by K. Wilson)

Hand traverses

A true hand traverse is an extremely strenuous move along a line of hand holds with nothing at all for the feet. Fortunately these moves are rare and most hand traverses have a slab of rock below on which the feet can be placed. Any friction on the feet, however small, will relieve the intolerable strain on the arms.

20 A classic hand traverse. Direct Route on Glyder Fach, north Wales. (Photograph by K. Wilson)

Years ago we used to practise hand traversing across the brick facing of a railway tunnel on a seldom used branch line. You had to move fast in order to complete the crossing before your strength ran out. We found it easier to have our heads at hand level with our elbows crooked rather than to hang down at full stretch. If you heard the whistle of a train it was a great spur to complete the traverse before your eyes and throat became engulfed in smoke.

Traverses

Traversing across a rock face rather than making a vertical ascent is a very different exercise. No strength is needed to pull the body up, it is all a question of balance. A wider variety of holds can be used on traverses because side holds assume great importance. On a steep wall traverse try and keep moving and vary your hand holds to use different muscles, this will save your fingers from becoming too tired. If foot holds are scarce you may have to change feet, a little skip is the method I use to accomplish this but it is vital to look down and see exactly what you are doing. There is no room for error because side holds by themselves will not support the weight of a climber.

If you are about to tackle a traverse pitch and you are climbing in a rope of three, make sure that the weakest member of the party is the middle man. The leader and third man will get little or no protection from the rope if they fall and they could suffer a nasty, grazing, pendulum swing. The middle man however can be held from each side.

A girdle traverse is a complete traverse of a rock face from one side to the other. Such climbs are particularly popular on outcrops where long traverses involving several pitches may be possible. Some ascent and descent may be necessary when the level of the traverse line changes.

Rock climbing practice

Wherever you live you should find it possible to get some rock climbing practice. If you live in the hills there is no problem, for real rocks provide the best practice grounds of all. New sports centres are mushrooming up in many of our cities and a number of these have artificial climbing walls incorporated into their structure. These are usually brick or concrete block walls, up to 40 feet, into which have been let boulders of hard rock. The boulders are spaced out at carefully calculated intervals to make climbing routes of different grades. In addition to the jutting out boulders, gaps and crevices have been made in the wall to provide additional holds. Corners, chimneys, cracks and even overhangs have been specially constructed in an attempt to reproduce the real thing.

Although climbing walls are undoubtedly instructive and can provide amusement on a wet afternoon, I have never liked them. For me rock climbing means the ascent of naturally occurring cliffs. I need the atmosphere, the weather, the sense of touch and smell and the views, stimuli which can never be found indoors.

Explore your locality. You will probably find an old quarry, rock outcrop or wall which can give you some useful practice and some fun. Sea cliffs are rapidly being developed as climbers' playgrounds. You don't need a partner or a rope if you stick to traverse lines near the ground. When your strength runs out just jump down. Such climbs will teach you a lot about balance, different holds and your own muscular stamina. They will also strengthen your fingers, wrists and arms and are a much better way of keeping fit than doing press-ups.

Don't attempt to climb on buildings. It may seem to you to be a clever and courageous act to place a chamber pot on the local church steeple but this is sheer stupidity. You may have heard of the 'Night Climbers of Cambridge', a group of undergraduate climbers who performed daring acts before the war, but you will not have heard of their horrific accident rate. Two years before I went up to Oxford a young climber was killed in a fall from the overhang on the Radcliffe Camera. A friend of mine from Brasenose College saw the imprint of the body in the lawn and was physically sick.

Try to remember that rock climbing is only one part of the magnificent sport of greater mountaineering. Don't jeopardize a lifetime's pleasure amongst the mountains by one careless or foolhardy act whilst rock climbing.

21 An artificial climbing wall.

22　Practising on Finiston Dock wall. (Photograph by K. Wilson)

3 Snow and Ice Climbing

Most mountain ranges are covered with snow for at least part of the year and you cannot call yourself a complete mountaineer unless you can move safely across snow fields and glaciers. In the Alps and the Himalayas snow climbing may make up nearly all the actual ascent and even in Britain you can find yourself having to cope with snow and ice in the most unexpected places, and at unusual times.

Small snow fields last throughout the year in several gullies and north-facing corries in Scotland, the most renowned being the north faces of Ben Nevis and Braeriach. The exceptionally hot summers of 1959 and 1976 have possibly been the only occasions this century when these two snow fields have actually disappeared. I like to think that perhaps even in these years some small patch of snow did remain unmelted somewhere in Scotland and that perpetual snow does lie in Britain. Climatologists have calculated that if the summit plateau of Ben Nevis was to be raised 600 feet to a height of 5000 feet the snow fields there would be permanent. In winter in the Highlands of Scotland the snow on the tops builds up to reach maximum depth in mid-April. In 1884 the maximum depth of snow on the summit of Ben Nevis was 12 feet as late as 28 May.

On the hills of Britain snow can fall on every day of the year and although I do not suggest that you arm yourself with ice axe and crampons in the summer months, even then snow and iced rocks can occasionally force a retreat. One early June day in Scotland I was walking across the remote mountainous area north of Loch Maree when a cold front passed over. The temperature dropped rapidly and torrential rain fell, which soon turned to sleet and then to snow. Three inches of snow fell in as many hours and I struggled up iced rocks and over treacherously slippery snow slopes to gain my objective, a peak called Ruadh Stac Mhor at 3014 feet. I had started out in warm sunny weather and had not thought to bring an ice axe, gloves or balaclava. My face became crusted with ice and my hands numb, and it was with great relief that I slid and floundered down the mountainside to the shelter of the valley. By the end of the day the clouds had passed over and the sun was out and, looking back, the mountains appeared white and sparkling against the blue sky. I marvelled at the beauty and contrast and I realized that even after twenty years of climbing, the mountains could still surprise me with their rapidly changing moods.

Winter mountaineering brings its own rewards and many of my most memorable days in the hills have been during the winter months. Personally I find winter mountaineering one of the great pleasures of life. A fine day in winter or preferably in early spring when the days are longer produces clear sharp air and excellent visibility and snow can make the ascent of a modest mountain a real challenge. Your boots crunch through frozen puddles as you approach the mountain and you tramp easily over the cast-iron bogs on the lower slopes. Higher up the mountain you kick steps up the snow and if patches of ice are met you strap on crampons, rope up for safety and cut steps. The cold air is soon forgotten and all your concentration is needed to ensure a safe ascent.

As you approach the summit ridge or plateau the slope steepens and you may have to cut your way through an overhanging lip of snow called a cornice. Finally, you emerge triumphant into the sunshine on the plateau and the panorama opens up to give magnificent views. Under conditions such as these the mountains of Britain can rival any in the world for beauty and such days are unforgettable. You are in a different world, a

fairyland of sparkling snow crystals and frost feathers, a world which only mountaineers can ever know. However, climbing mountains in winter is always more difficult and dangerous than in summer and the margin of safety is far less. It is essential to be well equipped and to allow plenty of time to deal with unforeseen conditions.

The ice axe

One April day a few years ago I set out with my son, Tim, who was twelve years old, to climb Snowdon. It had been a hard and late winter and fresh snow had recently fallen on the hills. Snowdon, blanketed in white and set against a blue sky, looked irresistible but I knew the conditions would be hard and so I selected the Pyg track from Pen-y-Pass which, in summer, is one of the major tourist routes up the mountain.

Soon after leaving Lyn Llydaw we were walking in soft snow and there was no trace of the path. We felt true pioneers plodding through the virgin snow and we made good speed until we reached the final 500 feet of steep slopes leading to the col between Snowdon and Crib-y-ddysgl. At this point the thin covering of snow lay over sheets of hard ice and we had to clear the snow and cut steps in the ice to give adequate security. Cutting steps with an ice axe is tiring but exhilarating work and we regularly swopped over the lead. We felt relaxed and satisfied as we gained the col high above the frozen Llyn Glaslyn and sat down for lunch watching a large party of students on the slopes below about to start climbing the steep section.

The students had no ice axes and when they reached the sheet ice they got into all kinds of trouble. With much shouting and slithering, they attempted to use our footsteps but one girl lost her grip and shot down the slope taking several others of the party with her. Of course without axes they had no hope of arresting their fall and they slammed into a pile of snow-covered rocks at the bottom. Miraculously they did not appear to be hurt and the rest of the party retreated gingerly and slunk away down

the mountain. It could so easily have been a fatal accident and I could not help contrasting their unhappy and dangerous day's climbing with that of Tim and I. We successfully made it to the summit of Snowdon and descended down the railway track to Half Way Station, and thence down into the Llanberis Pass. Even the railway track was snowed over with hard snow set at a steep angle and would have been a treacherous route for the ill prepared.

This story illustrates one of the most important rules of winter mountaineering, 'Always bring an ice axe'. If possible buy your own ice axe. A good one will last many years and when, through use, it is brown and scratched, it will become an old friend that has accompanied you on many conquests. Like a rope, an ice axe is a vital piece of safety equipment and if you borrow one you cannot be sure of its past history and its weaknesses are not easily detected. Before I deal with the subject of selection of an ice axe, I will mention some of its many uses in the mountains. These are belaying in snow, step cutting, assisting in balance when traversing steep slopes, cutting down cornices, clearing ice from rocks, arresting a slip on steep snow and ice slopes, probing the snow for hidden crevasses, braking when glissading downhill and screwing in ice pitons.

Nowadays there are different types of ice axe made for different purposes and you will probably have seen short alloy axes with wicked looked spikes hanging up in climbing shops. A short axe is ideal for near vertical ice gullies and north walls but it is useless as a general purpose axe. Select a sound Austrian axe with an ash shaft between 70- and 110-centimetres long. The length depends on the height of the climber but a rough guide is that when held at the pick end by a person standing straight up the end should just touch the ground. An ice axe should not be too light or it will not carry enough momentum as it is swung to cut a step, and equally important it should feel balanced. When you have bought your axe be sure to write your name on it immediately; I have found that poker work using a red hot skewer to be a satisfactory method. Before you put your ice axe away for the summer, lightly grease the metal parts and rub down the shaft with a rag soaked in linseed oil.

23 Advanced Alpine climbing. The Walker Spur of the Grandes Jorasses. (Photograph by D. Scott)

Don't misuse your ice axe. I once used mine for chopping wood outside the remote Shenavall bothy in Scotland, broke the shaft and made a fool of myself. I had to miss the following day's climbing too.

Your ice axe may come fitted with a wrist sling or you may wish to purchase a sling and fit it yourself. Opinion in the climbing world is divided on the question of ice axe slings. There are those who say that the merits of the sling are outweighed by the danger of injury in an uncontrolled fall caused by a flailing ice axe attached to the wrist. However, I find a sling immensely useful when climbing mixed rock and ice routes, for both hands can be used for the rock sections while the axe dangles from my wrist, yet the axe is always at hand to clear away snow and ice when necessary. My advice is to start by using a sling, for when you are not yet accustomed to an ice axe, it is easy to knock it against a rock and lose hold of it. Later you can decide for yourself (*see fig. 24*).

Most rucksacks have provision for attaching ice axes but, although this is useful for approach marches, when you are actually on hills in winter the right place for your ice axe is in your hand. Many accidents have occurred to parties who have met a patch of snow and have not bothered to remove their ice axes from their rucksacks, preferring to attempt a crossing without. When out on the mountains with an inexperienced party, I always insist that everyone has his ice axe at the ready at the first sight of snow. I enjoy carrying an ice axe in my hand, it gives me an added sense of purpose, it helps me balance when crossing boulder fields and its familiar note as it strikes a rock is music to my ears.

When you reach a steep snow slope that is sufficiently soft for you to kick steps up, don't make a bee-line for the top but try to work out a possible route, taking the line of easiest angle. If the top of the slope joins a ridge or plateau it may be corniced and you should seek a way round the corniced sections. Of course if you are climbing a gully with steep walls, you have little choice of route.

Zig-zag your way up the slope holding your axe in the hand nearest the snow (*see fig. 25*). This means that every time you change direction you have to change hands, but if your feet slip away you will find that you

instinctively lean into the slope, your weight will drive the axe into the snow and you will slide only a few inches. It is vital to arrest a slip immediately, for once you have gathered speed it is much harder to stop.

On a particularly steep slope it is advisable to force the ice axe into the snow before making a new step in readiness for a slip. Do remember to stand well away from the slope to keep your centre of gravity over your feet in exactly the same way as you would when climbing a slab of rock. If you hug the snow your feet are much more likely to push snow down the slope causing the footsteps to break away.

Fig. 24 Ice axe

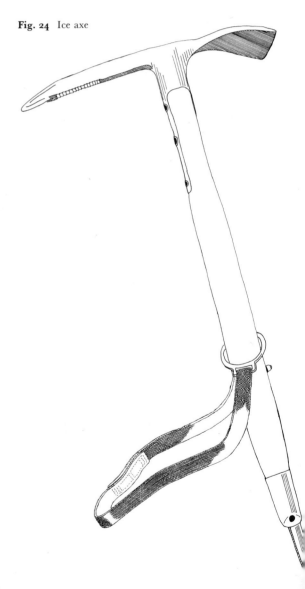

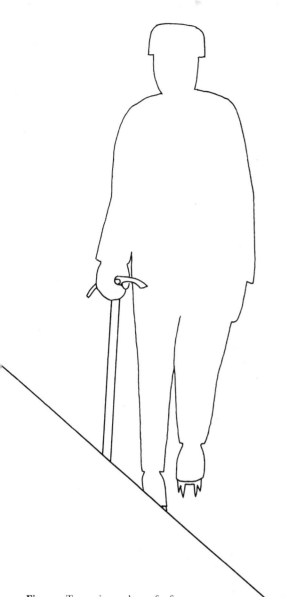

Fig. 25 Traversing a slope of soft snow

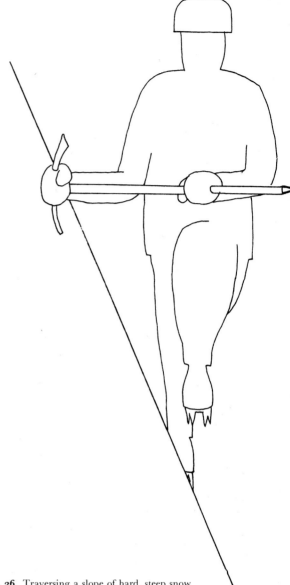

Fig. 26 Traversing a slope of hard, steep snow

If the snow is too hard for the ice axe to be inserted very far, or if the surface of the snow is glazed with ice, you must adopt a different technique. Hold the ice axe across the body, one hand firmly grasping the pick and the other the shaft (*as in fig. 26*). The pick should be nearest the snow/ice so that if a slip occurs the pick can be driven hard into the snow with the weight of your body behind it.

In view of the unpredictable nature of snow and the many different conditions encountered, you are bound sooner or later to have a slide. The drill for arresting a slide is simple and effective, and its execution must become second

nature. As soon as you slip, roll over onto your front and grasp your ice axe in the position shown in fig. 27 with one hand firmly grasping the adze. Don't hold your ice axe at arm's length for it may either be torn from your grasp or else not have sufficient weight over it to bite deeply enough into the snow to stop your fall. It is essential to prevent a jerk by allowing the pick to gradually bite deeper into the snow as it absorbs the energy of the moving body.

Find some steepish snow with a safe run out at the bottom and practise the routine until you are sure you can stop yourself effectively. By

Such snow is very common in Britain in March and April. To climb hard snow you must cut out steps with an ice axe or wear crampons, or sometimes use a combination of both.

Step cutting is a technique which takes much practice to perfect. To begin with you will probably seize the ice axe with both hands and hew out broad platforms at widely spaced intervals; I know I did. However, your arms will soon become tired, you will become bathed in sweat and you will find that as you mantleshelf from platform to platform your progress is exceedingly slow. Ideally one carefully measured full swing of the axe should be enough to make a nick which is large enough to take your boot. But this will depend on the consistency of the snow and a patch of hard ice may need many blows with the point of the axe using both hands to strike with enough force. The steps you make should be no further apart than if you were kicking them. When step cutting it is important to conserve energy and to maintain rhythm, and reaching out for steps not only breaks rhythm and leaves you panting but throws you off balance.

Do make sure that the steps you cut are in firm snow which will take your weight. A common condition which one finds is a light layer of powder snow laid on a surface of ice. This is particularly treacherous and is best left alone until you are more experienced. If it is absolutely vital to cross such a slope, take your time, clear the snow from each step and cut deeply into the ice with your axe.

Before you start on a proper climb find a bank of snow or a frozen waterfall and practise cutting a few steps.

Cornices

In winter cornices form above many slopes and corries. High winds blow snow across exposed plateaus and ridges, and build it up again in huge masses which overhang the leeward slopes. I have often seen cornices jutting out for 20 feet or more above the cliffs of Ben Nevis or in the Cairngorms. In early summer a typical view of the Highlands includes white wreaths of old cornices still in position below the ridges, a legacy of the winter snows.

When you are walking along a corniced ridge be very careful to keep well away from the

Fig. 27 The correct position for arresting a slide down steep snow

doing so you will gain confidence and be able to enjoy moving safely over snow. When practising this technique, however, be sure to wear gloves because crystalline snow can be as hard and as rough as sandpaper, and your hands can get skinned.

In early spring patches of old snow can become extremely hard and icy. This is because the surface is melted by the sun during the day, but it freezes again during the night. Successive meltings and freezings leads to the formation of hard snow up which steps cannot be kicked.

edge. From above it is not easy to gauge the distance which a cornice juts out and many accidents have occurred through climbers under-estimating this distance and falling through the snow or causing the cornice to break away. Fig. 28 gives an indication of the possible line of break of a cornice and you will notice how low it is. A safe traverse line would be well down on the left-hand side.

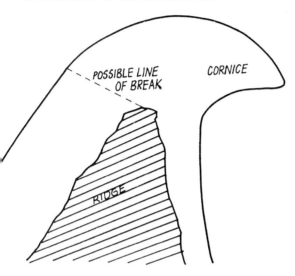

Fig. 28 The possible line of break of a cornice

The most difficult but exciting part of a snow climb is the approach to the cornice from below. If you are climbing a gully the cornice blocks off the sky and as you ascend the shadowy and ever steepening slopes, adrenalin starts coursing through your veins. By now the angle will be sufficiently high for you to need handholds as well as footholds. In soft snow you can plunge in one arm as far as the shoulder to maintain your balance while, with the ice axe held in the other hand, you can lean back and hack away at the cornice. In hard snow you must use the axe to chip out incut holds for your hands. Whichever method you use the assault on a cornice is always exhausting.

It may be that the cornice overhangs too far for it to be cut away and in this case you must tunnel through it and emerge onto the plateau or ridge through a hole in the snow. Large amounts of snow will certainly have to be shifted and most of it will fall on top of your poor companion belayed below you down the

24 Surmounting a cornice above Black Spout gully, Lochnagar.

slope. Spare him a thought as he cowers, shivering, on his stance with his anorak hood done up tightly in a vain effort to keep out the powder snow. At last you emerge into the sunshine, fix a belay and bring up your second. Together you can share the sense of achievement from the climb and the unique beauty of the mountains in winter.

61

25 Cornice on Y-Garn, north Wales. Soon after this photograph was taken a climber fell through the cornice and was seriously injured.

Belaying in snow and ice

When climbing on snow and ice that is not too difficult, it is usual practice for the party to be roped up but to move together. This technique has been developed for Alpine climbing when long days on snow and ice can be expected and there is just not sufficient time to move individually as in rock climbing. The technique is adequate precaution against a member of the party falling into a crevasse or sliding away out of control down a slope, but it should be used with circumspection. When in doubt make proper belays and move individually. In Britain with novice climbers I have only rarely used the moving together technique, preferring either to move solo or to use rope work as described in the rock climbing chapter. However, an inexperienced party can derive much confidence from the rope and I will describe its use.

A party of four should rope up at 10-metre intervals using a single 40-metre rope. The climbers can either tie on using a figure of eight knot clipped into their waist belts, or harnesses, or they can arrange the same knot directly round their waists. Keeping about four metres apart, the climbers should hold a few short coils of rope in the lower hand, which does not hold the ice axe, and thereby take up the slack. It is the responsibility of each climber to ensure that slack does not accumulate in front of him causing the climber ahead to stumble or trip. Coils are let out or taken in as necessary.

If one of the party slips he should immediately shout a warning to the others, who must plunge their ice axes as far as possible into the snow and hang on tight. When you are more experienced you may find it more efficient always to have a turn of the rope round the ice axe shaft so that when the axe is thrust into the snow the friction of the rope will gradually absorb the force of the falling body and the axe is less likely to be jerked out. To begin with,

26 A classic Scottish ridge – the Aonach Eagach. (Photograph by D. Bennet)

though, you will find it takes all your concentration to keep your distance from the climber in front and to manage efficiently the coils of rope.

If you and your companion are roped together and are traversing a narrow ridge of powder snow and your companion falls off, immediate and drastic action must be taken. Snow plumed to a razor edge is not likely to be compact enough to take an ice axe belay and so you must take the only way open to you, which is to jump down the other side of the ridge! As the rope becomes tight the weight of your bodies counter-balance each other, the fall is arrested and you can both climb back to regain the crest of the ridge.

The thought of jumping down the side of a ridge is horrifying but if the need should ever arise you would have only a split second to act, and I am sure you would do it. I was once descending from the summit of the Allalinhorn,

a 4000-metre peak in the Swiss Alps, and I was roped to a girl with much enthusiasm but little experience. The ridge was razor sharp and the snow was deep powder over hard ice. For twenty metres I kicked away the snow and cut deep steps in the ice, I then straddled the ridge *à cheval*, took in the slack rope and called her to join me. Suddenly she missed one of the steps and on her back shot down towards the glacier 3000 feet below. Without thinking, I threw myself down the other, equally steep, side and sure enough the technique worked and both our lives were saved. I am sure you would have done the same. I am not suggesting that such an occurrence is likely to befall you but even on classic ridges in Britain such as Crib Goch on Snowdon, or the Aonach Eagach in Glen Coe, such emergencies could arise in winter and it is essential to know what to do.

When climbing on steep snow and ice you should use stances, belays and running belays as you would for rock climbing. To make a belay in snow first of all carve out a good ledge on which to stand and then drive your ice axe into the snow well above the stance, at least as high as shoulder level. If you can get the axe in to the hilt so much the better, stamp on it if necessary, but if this proves to be impossible be sure to tie off the belay round the ice axe shaft at snow level. If you tie it at the pick end the extra leverage could snap the shaft or pull it out (*see fig. 29*).

If you are belaying on ice or extremely hard snow you must use an ice peg. These come in many different shapes and sizes but there are three main types (*see fig. 30*). Unless you set out specifically to climb an ice route you will have to select just one or two ice pegs to carry in case they are needed. I would recommend type 'b', which is the most versatile, but don't forget to bring a piton hammer to drive the peg into the ice and remember that it can easily be unscrewed using the ice axe pick. Before driving in the ice peg, cut a small ledge so the peg can penetrate the tough inside of the ice (*as in fig. 31*).

When using ice pegs as running belays insert them as described above but don't run the rope directly through a karabiner attached to the peg, this will cause drag on the rope. Use a sling and karabiner to keep the rope well clear.

Fig. 29 Tying off an ice axe belay

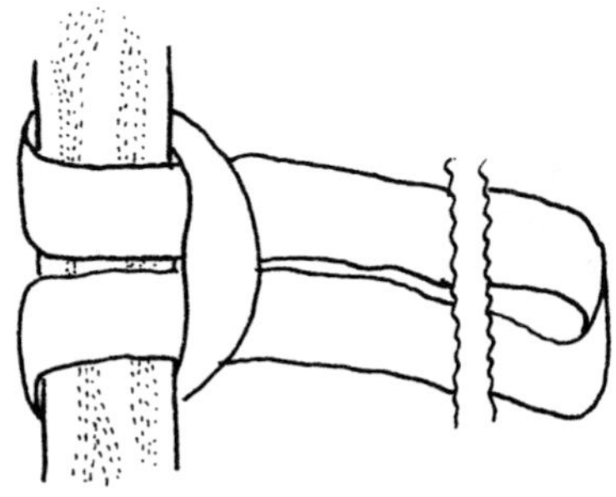

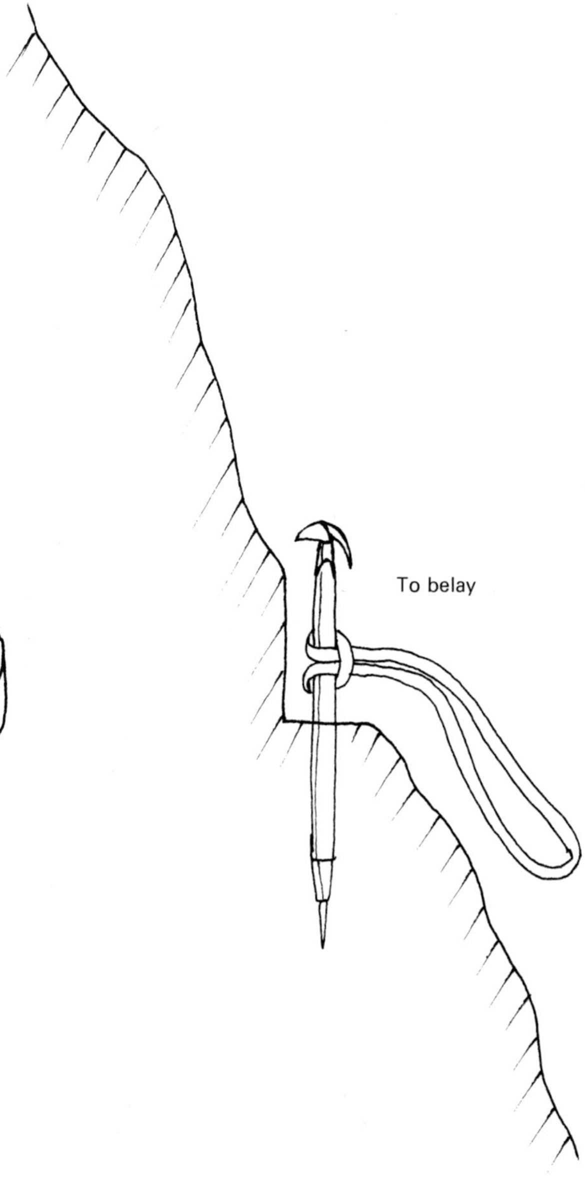

To belay

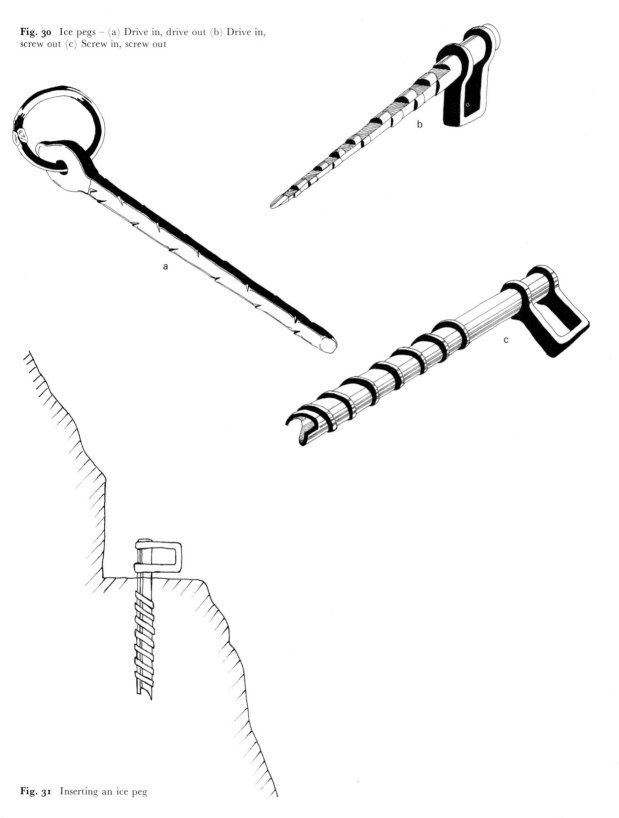

Fig. 30 Ice pegs – (a) Drive in, drive out (b) Drive in, screw out (c) Screw in, screw out

Fig. 31 Inserting an ice peg

The 'dead man' snow belay

As an alternative to the ice axe belay and as an essential belay in soft unconsolidated snow, the 'dead man' can be used. A 'dead man' is a strong aluminium plate about 10-inches across with holes in the middle to which a loop of wire is attached (*see fig. 32*). The 'dead man' acts as a snow anchor. It is buried such that the tension is applied at an angle of about 50° to the plane of the plate and provided that it is placed correctly, it will withstand a considerable load. As anyone making a snowball knows, snow has strange properties when compressed. It gives at first and then compacts and the give during the compression absorbs energy, making the 'dead man' an ideal belay.

A channel must be dug for the wire to emerge from the snow at the correct angle but snow can be packed around again when the 'dead man' is in position (*as in fig. 33*). The idea is that any sudden tension on the wire drives the 'dead man' deeper into the snow rather than pulling it out.

The 'dead man' is a fairly new piece of safety equipment and I must emphasize the importance of using it correctly. Again, only practice and experience will teach you the strengths and weaknesses of its use.

Fig. 33 Positioning the 'dead man'

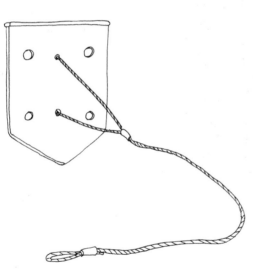

Fig. 32 The 'dead man' snow belay

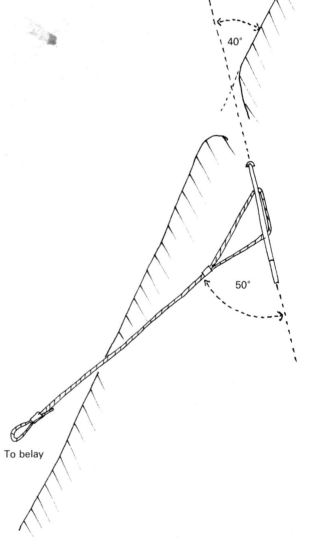

40°

50°

To belay

Crampons

The ordinary vibram-soled climbing boot is designed to grip rock and it is very unsatisfactory for steep snow and ice climbing. To get over this problem frameworks of steel spikes, called crampons, can be strapped onto boots and these will bite into the frozen surface, thus providing purchase. If you intend to enjoy winter mountaineering in safety, crampons will be an essential part of your equipment.

There are two main designs of crampon. First, ten pointers, four on the heel and six on the front part of the foot with all the points projecting vertically downwards. It is vital that the rear points are level with the heel of the boot and the front points are level with the toe.

Since there is little or no adjustment on these crampons, they should be carefully fitted to the boot at the time of purchase.

Second, there are lobster claw crampons which are essentially the same as those described above except that they have two front spikes projecting at an angle of 45°. Experienced ice climbers can ascend near vertical slopes with just these front claws digging into the ice. Several manufacturers make adjustable lobster claw crampons which can be fitted to any size of boot and I have used Salewa adjustables in Scotland and the Himalayas with utmost confidence (*see fig. 34*).

Fig. 34 Crampons – (a) Fixed ten pointers (b) Lobster claw adjustables

The great advantage of wearing crampons is that on steep snow an experienced climber can dispense with step cutting. At the beginning you should not rely on crampons alone, because they take some getting used to. On your first few climbs use crampons together with step cutting for extra security. When wearing crampons place the foot flat so that all ten points bite into the snow. You will find that using crampons in this way places great strain on the ankle and calf muscles but the extra feeling of security which they impart is wonderfully reassuring. Here are a few safety points to bear in mind when using them.

1 Walking in crampons means that you must pick your feet up higher than usual at every step, so it is very easy to stumble.

2 The points can catch in your socks, snow gaiters and breeches.

3 Take great care not to damage the climbing rope by treading on it with sharp crampon spikes.

4 A good rucksack will have a reinforced section sewn on to the flap for carrying crampons. Secure them with the points downwards.

5 When climbing on soft sugary snow, watch out for crampons 'balling up'. This occurs when snow sticks to the underside of the crampon and forms a solid mass or 'ball'. Instead of presenting ten spikes to the surface of the snow the only contact is snow with snow and little or no grip results. In conditions like these, the snow which adheres to them can be knocked off at regular intervals with a blow from the ice axe on the side of the foot.

Crampons can be heavy and awkward but don't be tempted to leave them behind and don't lose them for they can be life savers. Many years ago a party of four of us from university climbed the beautiful Dent d'Hérens in the Swiss Alps. The last 800 feet to the summit lay up hard smooth ice set at a high angle. In two ropes of two we cramponed up to the summit and lunched in the sunshine, enjoying a stupendous view from our 14,000-foot perch. One of the party took off his crampons to ease his feet and he inadvertently

dropped them down the north face. We watched them bounding down to the glacier 3000 feet below. Our descent of the mountain took many hours for we had to tie both climbing ropes together and literally lower our cramponless friend, whose boots made no impression on the ice, to the full extent of the ropes. He hacked himself out a stance in the ice while we gaily cramponed down to him and repeated the procedure until easier ground was reached.

Avalanches

Avalanches are large masses of snow, usually in layers, which slide downhill and in the Alps and Himalayas they present a major hazard to the climber. It is not generally realized that avalanches occur every year in Britain and many climbers in England, Scotland and Wales have been avalanched because they did not appreciate the danger. I myself have occasionally seen an avalanche occurring in Scotland and a very frightening experience it is. The first warning is a crack, followed by a low rumble, which increases to a roar as the snow thunders down. If you become a winter mountaineer you are bound to see avalanche debris at the bottom of snow slopes and gullies even if you do not witness one taking place.

The cause of avalanches is lack of cohesion between layers, whether it is snow on ice or snow on a different type of snow. It is very difficult to predict avalanches so it is essential to err on the side of safety. Skiers are often frustrated by danger notices put up by the authorities on seemingly harmless slopes of snow.

A lot of research has been done on avalanches and I do not intend to go deeply into the science of the structure of snow, but here are a few guidelines.

1 Keep away from slopes of fresh powder snow which have not had time to consolidate.

2 Beware of deep snow which has become rotten following a sudden thaw.

3 Look out for the 'wind slab' condition. This is the formation of a thin crust of hard snow by successive meltings and freezings of the surface, the snow underneath remaining powdery and unconsolidated. The surface slab can easily break away and avalanche.

You do get some warnings of 'wind slab' conditions. If your boot breaks through the surface crust of snow at every step, sending pieces of hard slab skidding down the hillside, beware of 'wind slab'.

4 Remember that it is the snow conditions that cause avalanches; if these conditions are right even quite gentle slopes can avalanche.

Glissading

The descent from mountains under winter conditions can be a very pleasurable experience. It is often possible to romp down snow fields at great speed making for the valley bottom and a well-earned tea. The snow cushions each step and you avoid the jarring of the knees that can occur in summer. Tiresome slopes of scree and boulders are buried under the snow, and if you get out of control there is a soft landing and only the jeers of your companions to contend with as you shake the snow out of your hair.

You may be lucky enough to meet slopes of hard, firm snow down which you can glissade. A glissade is a controlled slide on the feet, somewhat akin to skiing without skis. But as with all mountaineering practice it must be done properly. Don't lie on your back or sit on a slippery anorak, or cagoule, for by doing so you have little view of where you are going and even less control. Squat down with your feet facing down the slope, your ice axe held to one side and the ice axe spike pressing into the surface of the snow. By decreasing or increasing the pressure on your axe you can control your speed and at the same time remain in balance (*see fig. 35*).

I shall never forget my best ever glissade one March day in Scotland. We had climbed Ben Nevis by the classic Tower Ridge route in the morning and then traversed a knife-edged arête to the summit of Carn Mor Dearg at 3999 feet. Below in the glen was the tiny climbing hut where we were staying and a long tongue of hard snow led from the summit cairn to the hut itself. In no more than ten minutes we had swooped down the snow to the hut in an exhilarating 2000-foot standing glissade.

It is very tempting after a long day out on the hills to descend recklessly and there are three vital safety rules which you must adhere to before your flight to the valley.

1 Always have your ice axe at the ready. The softest snow can turn to sheet ice with no warning.

2 Always check that the slope down which you are glissading ends in a gentle run out of snow or grass. In your exuberance it is only too easy to plunge headlong over cliffs or into rocks.

3 Be very careful not to wave your ice axe in the air. It is a dangerous weapon and it could easily cause injury to yourself or to your companions.

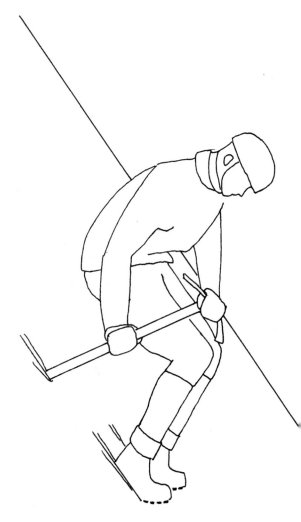

Fig. 35 The snow glissade

Descents are not always easy and you should allow time for setbacks and enforced changes of plan. I once climbed a 3000-foot mountain in Kintail called Ciste Dubh. It was early spring and I was by myself and the south ridge, heavily iced and corniced, gave me a challenging climb. As I left the summit cairn to descend gentle slopes to the glen I realized that the entire mountain was sheeted in hard ice. I did not fancy returning by the south ridge and I had foolishly left my crampons behind. There was no alternative but to start step cutting and by the time I had reached easy ground I was hot, hungry and very annoyed with myself. I only just made it back to the car before nightfall.

In Britain the weather patterns are so complex that almost every type of snow and ice condition can be met with, sometimes on the same day. It is this broad experience coupled with the toughness gained by climbing in near Arctic conditions that makes the Scottish climber such a force in the Alps and Himalayas.

I hope by now I have encouraged you to venture out onto the hills in winter. The special techniques required for snow and ice climbing cannot satisfactorily be learnt from a book. Buy an ice axe, go out this winter to some easy hills and learn for yourself.

4 Equipment

Proper equipment is the key to maximum enjoyment and adequate safety. First and foremost the piece of equipment should do the job for which it was designed and secondly, for ease of carrying over the mountains it should be as light as possible. It is common to see parties of walkers, with faces set in grim determination, carrying huge rucksacks along mountain paths. This is admirable if their intention is to use the mountains as a testing ground for their fitness but they cannot get much enjoyment out of their walk nor can they appreciate, with sweat pouring into their eyes, all that the hills have to offer.

Of course a certain minimum amount of equipment must always be carried, enough to cope with any emergency and to ward off the bad weather that can arise in the mountains at a moment's notice. But for hill walking in summer the essentials can be pared down to a few items which can be easily and fairly cheaply bought. The possession of a comfortable pair of boots, warm clothes, waterproofs, map and compass and a rucksack enables a climber to range far and wide over the hills. It is true to say though that the price of mountaineering equipment is proportional to the quality and usefulness of that equipment, and as you graduate to harder climbs on higher mountains you must be prepared to pay more. If you fail to do this your enjoyment will be impaired and safety margin reduced.

Personal clothing and equipment

Let us begin by considering personal clothing, starting at the feet.

Boots (*see fig. 36*)
When you are choosing a pair of boots aim above all for comfort. It is not enough to take a few steps on the shop floor carpet before making your decision. Remember that the boots will be worn across boulder fields and scree slopes of sharp stones, across acid peat bogs and they will be required to grip in steep, snow-filled gullies and on wet, lichen-encrusted rocks. No mountaineering boots can be completely waterproof but check for the following points:

1 The tongue should be padded and sewn right up the instep.

2 The laces should either fasten round cleats or pass through metal 'D' rings, not through eyelets.

3 The leather should be in one piece with no exposed stitching. Raised threads are very vulnerable to the abrasive action of stones and the corrosive action of acid peat bogs.

4 The inside of the boot should not be lined with wool or fur because linings soon wear away completely.

5 The uppers should be padded and high enough to cover the ankle bone.

6 The soles should be of vibram rubber which is tough and has a high degree of friction. For general mountain use the sole should be thick and flexible. When you are carrying a heavy rucksack your feet are susceptible to bruising from sharp stones and a thick and well-insulated sole will help to prevent this happening.

7 If you want a pair of boots which will be suitable for both rock climbing and Alpine climbing, the sole will need to be stiffened. When you are balancing on small toe holds the sole must not bend, and Alpine boots have a shank of steel or wood running three-quarters of the way (and sometimes the whole way) along the sole between the vibram outer and the leather inner. Alpine boots are not very suitable for walking because the lack of flexibility in the sole means that the heel rides up and down at every step and this can lead to bruising and blisters.

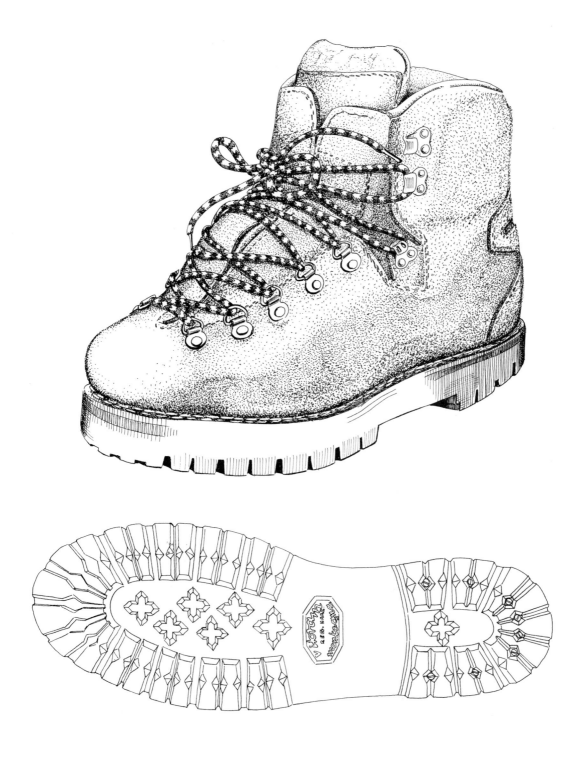

Fig. 36 General purpose mountaineering boots and
vibram soles

8 Climbing boots should not cramp the toes because, apart from the discomfort this causes, in cold weather the restricted circulation of the blood could lead to frost-bite. Even when wearing two pairs of socks you should be able to wriggle your toes inside your boots, but there should not be so much room that your feet slide up and down.

Never wear an extra pair of socks just to make a badly chosen pair of boots fit. But if you have a low instep you may find that insoles will help your feet to fit snugly.

New boots are usually hard and stiff and it is essential to break them in before you leave for the mountains. Wear the boots about the house and on short walks, and they will soon mould themselves to your feet. Wet boots should be stuffed with newspaper and dried very slowly in a well-ventilated room; they must never be baked in front of a fire. I use dubbin to keep the leather soft and pliable, but if you need the ankle support provided by firm uppers, you should use only shoe polish to condition the leather.

Nailed boots, which were extremely popular for rock climbing fifty years ago, should never now be worn. Hard nails rapidly wear away the small but vital holds on certain types of rock, while sloping holds become glazed and polished. For this reason, in recent years, many popular routes have been up-graded.

For specialized rock climbing you can wear patent lightweight boots called PAs or EBs (*see fig. 37*). These boots have very thick rubber soles which are slightly flexible, smooth but have high frictional properties. They have ankle-length canvas uppers and they are designed for a close fit, thus only a single pair of thin socks should be worn. The complete absence of a welt means that when standing on a small hold, more of your actual foot is over the hold, thereby transmitting pressure vertically downwards onto the rock. They are superb for climbing delicate slabs and they are a necessity for hard modern routes. The main disadvantage of PAs is that they can be used only for rock climbing, they are painful to wear for walking more than a very short distance. The usual practice is to walk to the cliff in big boots and change into PAs or EBs before starting the climb.

Fig. 37 The EB rock boot

A friend of mine once set out to climb the south face of the Marmolata, a long rock route in the Dolomites. The climb finishes at the summit of the Marmolata which, at 11,000 feet, is one of the highest peaks in the Dolomites and it holds a considerable glacier. A cable car runs from near the summit to the valley so, enticed by the thought of an easy descent, he decided to wear PAs for the entire expedition. But when he had completed the climb he found that the cable car was out of action and he was forced to make an excruciating descent to the valley on foot. He lost most of his toe nails and ruined the rest of his holiday.

Socks

One of the great advantages of wool is that it retains heat even when wet. Wool is softer than man-made fibres and woollen socks help to cushion the feet, so you should aim to wear two pairs. If you are wearing climbing breeches you will need thick woollen stockings as the outer pair, long enough to meet the short legs of the breeches which fasten just below the knee. It is possible to buy woollen stockings in many attractive colours and patterns. Loop-stitched stockings are particularly warm. The inside pair of socks can be of much softer and lighter material but keep to wool or a wool/terylene mixture. Nylon socks are not satisfactory since they encourage sweating, do not retain heat and, by sticking to the feet when damp, may cause blisters.

Gaiters

Snow gaiters, which reach to just below the knee, are essential for winter mountaineering. They keep snow out of your boots, they prevent your woollen stockings becoming clogged with snow and ice, and they provide an extra layer of insulation. Gaiters are made of canvas or nylon, but nylon is preferable because it absorbs less water and so is less likely to freeze up and become stiff. For ease of removal it is worth paying a little more to buy a pair of gaiters which zip up at the back. Many hill walkers have taken to wearing gaiters in all seasons. Undoubtedly they are useful for walking over wet and boggy ground but I find that in the summer months they are too hot and itchy to be worthwhile.

Trousers

For ease and freedom of movement when hill walking and rock climbing, it is important to wear loose-fitting trousers. Climbing breeches are baggy and they provide enough surplus material round the knees to avoid restriction when taking a high step or a long stride. Tweed breeches are superbly warm and hard wearing, and they are ideal for winter mountaineering. I usually wear an old pair of pyjama trousers under my breeches and, with this combination, I have never suffered from cold legs. 'Long Johns' instead of pyjamas are even warmer. 'Moleskin' breeches made of brushed cotton are softer but not quite so warm. Cord breeches are tough but rather hard and they can cause chaffing of the skin.

An old pair of cavalry twill trousers will be quite warm enough for summer climbing but light cotton jeans provide almost no protection against wind and rain, and are quite unsuitable. Don't wear shorts unless the weather is settled fine and you are not planning to go high.

Rock climbers are not noted for their desire to climb on high and remote cliffs, they generally prefer the low-lying crags, the nearer the road the better. Under these conditions it is safe to wear almost anything, jeans and T-shirts being very popular.

Anoraks and waterproofs

The all-round mountaineer probably values his anorak above any other item of personal equipment except his boots. The anorak provides above the waist protection against wind and rain, and often against cold as well. It does not really matter much what is worn under the anorak so long as it provides warmth and insulation. A vest, a shirt or two, old jerseys thick or thin and perhaps a tracksuit top all help to trap layers of air which insulate the body from the cold. However, no amount of shirts or jerseys will keep out the wind and rain and, on the high tops, these are the killers.

During my mountaineering career I have tested anoraks made of many different materials and on a number of occasions I have suffered from inferior garments. Lightweight cagoules of thin proofed nylon are adequate only for mild summer showers; they are quite useless for the heavy wind-driven rain which is commonly met with in the mountains. If you are wearing inadequate clothing and you get soaked to the skin your day will be ruined, for it will be essential to move down to lower ground as quickly as possible. Wind causes rapid evaporation from wet clothing and skin, and this in turn causes rapid cooling. Thus, for the ill-equipped, there is danger of hypothermia even in the summer.

Climbers have been slow to learn the lessons of yachtsmen and lifeboatmen. Like climbers, these men operate in cold and wet conditions but, they wear oilskins which are completely waterproof. Oilskins or nylon anoraks proofed with neoprene, and having welded seams, are not too expensive and they do the job perfectly well. Their unpopularity amongst climbers arises because the material does not breathe and condensed perspiration makes them damp and clammy. But surely it is better to be warm and clammy than soaked to the skin and frozen to the marrow. Ever since I bought my waterproof Helly Hansen suit, comprising anorak with hood and over-trousers, I have faced bad weather with equanimity. I only wish I had bought it twenty years earlier.

If you buy a neoprene proofed anorak you should also buy a pair of proofed over-trousers. Failure to do so will mean that rain running off your anorak will stream down onto your legs and saturate them very rapidly. Climbing breeches soak up a tremendous amount of water and are very difficult to dry out again.

Make sure that your anorak has a hood with

28 A winter day in the central Highlands.

draw strings and an outside pocket large enough for the map. There should be double thickness at the shoulders for strength and the cuffs should be elasticated. Check that your over-trousers are sufficiently wide at the bottom for them to be pulled over your boots.

The one material which is warm, windproof, waterproof and does breathe is proofed Ventile. Ventile is very closely woven Egyptian cotton, it is soft and hardwearing but it is extremely expensive. A new artificial fibre called Goretex has recently been developed in the United States. The manufacturers claim that it is absolutely waterproof on the outside yet it can breathe from the inside. If the claims are true Goretex will play an important future role in mountaineering clothing but I have heard that this new material is vulnerable to wear and it soon loses its efficiency.

Gloves

Even in summer it is worth carrying a pair of gloves. Snow can fall on the mountain tops in every month of the year and hands can quickly become numb. This could be dangerous as well as uncomfortable as you fumble with rucksack straps, zips, the map and the compass, while vital minutes are wasted. I recommend lightweight Damart Thermawear gloves with Dachstein wool mitts as a second pair for use in winter. For snow climbing you should wear proofed over-mitts to keep the inside pair dry.

Always wear an old pair of leather gloves when you are belaying another climber on a rock climb. In the event of a fall they will protect your hands from rope burns.

Headgear

It has been calculated that 30 per cent of the body's heat is lost through the head, thus it is vital to keep it well protected.

In wet weather pull up your anorak hood to prevent water trickling through your hair and into your collar. In winter you should wear a woollen balaclava helmet inside your anorak hood and if the weather is particularly severe you should put on a pair of goggles to protect your eyes from driving snow. Snow goggles or sunglasses should also be worn when you are climbing on snow or walking across a glacier in bright or sunny weather. The ultra-violet light reflected off the snow can cause the exceptionally painful condition known as snow blindness. You can guard against this for, like sunburn, it is avoidable.

Your clothing and equipment may be tested in winter even without precipitation. Powder snow underfoot can be whipped into blinding spicules which penetrate everything. At times I have been forced to turn away from the wind and bury my face in my gloved hands until the blast has passed. On occasions like these you are glad for the protection of a close-fitting balaclava and gloves which cover the wrists.

Safety helmets

For rock climbing and for steep snow and ice climbing you must wear a safety helmet. A high proportion of climbing accidents involve head injuries and unfortunately these are often the most serious. Head injuries can easily be sustained as the result of a fall as well as from avalanches or rock falls from above. Buy yourself a helmet conforming to British Standard 4423. These helmets have been especially designed to provide protection against sideways impacts as well as from above, while allowing freedom of sight, hearing and head movement.

Camping and backpacking equipment

Sleeping bags

A really good sleeping bag is more than a luxury, it is a necessity for high camping in the mountains. Whatever the hardships you have suffered during the day they should be forgotten at night when you snuggle down to enjoy a good night's sleep. Blankets are bulky and heavy, and quite impractical for camping. For summer nights under canvas and for Youth Hostels and climbing huts, a lightweight, fibre-filled sleeping bag will be adequate. But if you intend to camp high up in the mountains at all seasons of the year you must invest in a good down bag.

High quality duck or goose down is far better than any man-made fibre. It can be compressed to low bulk for ease of packing, it is light, it has a long life and it has excellent thermal efficiency. Although down is very expensive, remember that cold is sleep's worst enemy and the thicker the layer of down the warmer the sleeping bag. When you are lying in your sleeping bag your body compresses the down to a thin layer which does not provide very good insulation from the cold ground. Thus a down bag must always be used in conjunction with a foam pad or karrimat. These closed cell mats are very light, non-absorbent and comfortable. Air mattresses are much heavier, less practical and vulnerable to damage and I do not advise their use.

A down sleeping bag needs to be cared for. It must be kept clean and dry because wet down will never dry out to have the same efficiency as before. Down should be allowed to expand to its natural volume so the bag should not be stored in a tight roll but should be hung up vertically in the wardrobe. If you are not willing to pay for the luxury of a down bag buy one that is filled with natural fibre such as Dacron, P3 or Kapok. Although these fillings are bulky and heavy in comparison with down, the bags can also be warm, they are very tough and they may be washed without damage.

Whatever filling you choose for your sleeping bag make sure that it is either box or double quilted (see fig. 38). This keeps the filling evenly distributed and 'cold spots' are eliminated. Try to find a bag with a smooth and silky finish on the inside. This will allow you to turn over and wriggle around in your sleep without taking the bag with you.

Fig. 38 Box and double quilting

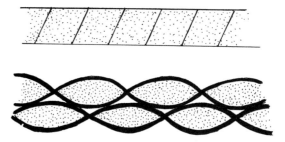

Zips are to be avoided. Whichever position you are in you always seem to be lying on the zip which digs into your ribs and lets in the cold.

Tents

The design of tents, following the development of new materials for use in their construction, has changed out of all recognition over the last twenty years. The heavy canvas tents, used for generations by the Army, youth clubs and scout troops, have given way to proofed cotton or Ventile tents with fly-sheets and these are now being rapidly superseded by ultra-lightweight tents of proofed nylon.

The choice is enormous and, unless you have had experience of camping in the mountains and know exactly the type of tent you need, the decision is hard to make. Before we consider the pros and cons of the different types of tent which are available, remember the two most important points of all. Firstly the tent must be 100 per cent weatherproof even to the extreme conditions experienced in the mountains. If water finds its way into the inner tent and soaks your sleeping bag and all your clothes you will probably have to return home immediately. Secondly, you must select a tent which is reasonably light because it will have to be backpacked into the mountains along with all your other climbing equipment and food.

Proofed cotton and Ventile is tough, weatherproof and warm. By using a fly-sheet you can live comfortably in the inner tent and you may touch the walls without dire results. The fly-sheet keeps the inner warm in winter, cool in summer and bears the brunt of the rain, snow and wind. The fabric can breathe and condensation is unknown. I have spent hundreds of comfortable and perfectly dry nights in a Blacks Mountain tent of proofed cotton but I must admit to one disadvantage: the tent is heavy and quite bulky and, in wet weather, it absorbs moisture (it is designed to do this so that the threads swell and close the pores) thereby increasing its weight by up to a half.

Tents constructed of polyurethane-proofed nylon are popular because they are light and quite cheap. If they are used with a fly-sheet they are waterproof. The major disadvantage of proofed nylon is that it does not breathe very well and condensation is a problem. Cooking inside the tent should be undertaken only as a last resort because it results in streams of water running down the walls, forming pools on the groundsheet and drips of water fall down your neck. If you touch the wet walls your shirt or jersey gets soaked.

In bad cases your moist breath will condense on the tent roof and by morning drops will be falling onto your sleeping bag. The problem is worse in winter when you cannot leave the tent flap open for air to circulate and sometimes the condensation freezes to hoar frost. In summer the warmer air can hold more moisture, and condensation can usually be avoided.

Nylon tents must be well aired every day and if the weather is fine your (damp) sleeping bag should be stretched out to dry, and to condition the down. Nylon as used for tents is a lightweight and thin material but it is surprisingly strong. Nevertheless make sure that your tent is of Rip-stop nylon which has heavy threads let into the material at closely spaced intervals to stop runs in the event of a tear. The built-in groundsheet takes a lot of wear and tear, and the nylon should be of far thicker gauge or even of PVC.

Nylon soaks up very little moisture so be sure to shake off the droplets from a wet tent and fly-sheet before stowing it away in your rucksack. At the end of your holiday hang up the tent in a well-aired room until it is thoroughly dry. This is particularly important for damp cotton tents which are prone to mildew and rot. Perhaps the best compromise is to buy a tent with a nylon fly-sheet and a cotton inner. This will be light, weatherproof and condensation-free.

Don't buy a tent with an integral fly-sheet; I once made the mistake of doing so with disastrous results. The tent's fly-sheet was attached to the inner at various points and when erected, there was a 2-inch air gap between the layers. The attraction was that in bad weather the tent could be erected in a very short time because there was no separate fly-sheet to bother about. But when wind and rain arrived, which it did on the first night, the pressure of the wind pushed the fly-sheet inwards so that it touched the inner tent. Within minutes rain was pouring through the side of the tent and as I wrung out my clothes

I realized that my purchase had been a dreadful mistake.

Here are a few points on the design of tents which you should watch out for.

1 'A' poles at the front and rear are much stronger than single poles and they allow for easy access.

2 A light alloy ridge pole will help to brace the tent and to keep the fly-sheet away from the inner in a strong wind.

3 Guy ropes come under considerable tension and when they are tied to boulders they can fray; for these reasons check that they are made from strong nylon cord. Don't use ropes of hemp or manilla because they shrink when wet and have to be slackened off.

4 Don't buy a tent that is too low. In winter when the days are short you will spend many hours in the tent and if you cannot sit up straight because of a low roof you will be very uncomfortable.

5 A tent with walls vastly increases the amount of space inside and a bell end at the rear provides a useful area for storage.

6 The front of the fly-sheet should zip right down to ground level making a windproof porch in which you can cook.

7 A flap or vallance running round the outside of the tent will be extremely useful for anchoring the tent in bad weather. Boulders or, in winter, snow, can be placed on the vallance to prevent the wind lifting the tent from underneath.

8 The fly-sheet should extend to ground level to prevent the wind lifting it off.

9 The tent entrance should have a good strong zip which can be manipulated from inside or out. Alternatively, and I prefer this, the tent should have a sleeve entrance which can be tied up securely from the inside.

10 Air vents should be let into the ends of the tent. This is particularly important for nylon tents since they help to prevent condensation. Check that the vents fasten securely because driving snow and spindrift can penetrate the smallest of holes.

11 Struggling to slot together tent pole sections by torchlight and in bad weather can be a nightmare. The section ends which fit together should be marked by a spot of coloured paint or a number code or, preferably, be linked by an elasticated cord or wire spring.

12 Steer clear of trendy designs which have not been thoroughly tested under all conditions.

On an expedition to Arctic Norway two boys in my party brought along a pneumatic tent with built-in inflatable ribs. While digging a drainage ditch around the tent with his ice axe, one boy punctured an important structural unit. The tent collapsed on the other boy who was inside lighting the primus. A gaping hole was burnt in the fabric of the roof and the tent was rendered useless.

Bivouacs
When you have gained experience of camping in the mountains and moving over high hill country, you may wish to experiment on your own with bivouacs or natural shelters. I once traversed the entire Cairngorm range from Glen Feshie in the south to Tomintoul in the north in three glorious summer days. My brother Christopher and I slept out every night in the heather with only a lightweight groundsheet for protection. It would have been safer and more comfortable to have taken a tent but our faithful Blacks Mountain weighed 15 pounds and was far too heavy for the job.

On another occasion, this time in winter, Alan (my friend and climbing companion) and I built a rough but roofed shelter of boulders, filled every cranny with packed snow, and survived several nights under the north face of Ben Nevis. Such practice would not now be necessary because proofed-nylon bivvy tents can be obtained which weigh less than 2 pounds. The mountain equipment firm of Karrimor sponsor an annual two-day mountain marathon. Competitors, in pairs, try to complete a demanding course over high mountainous country, calling in at various check points as they go and spending a compulsory night's camping at a predetermined site. The mandatory equipment list includes tent, sleeping bag, food, stove, spare clothes etc. I enjoy competing in this most popular event every year but I cannot match certain of my fellow competitors who manage to get the total weight of their rucksacks and contents down to below 6 pounds.

29 Winter on the north face of Ben Nevis.

Rucksacks

You will need two rucksacks. A lightweight day-sack to carry your lunch and spare clothes when you are walking or climbing in the mountains and a large sack, suitable for mountain camping and backpacking, when you will be carrying a considerable weight and bulk of equipment.

Let us deal first with the light rucksack. It should be showerproof at least and have an outside pocket for items of equipment which are needed at regular intervals such as compass, map and a bar of chocolate. Since you might use the rucksack for rock climbing, it must fit your back closely and it should not sag at the bottom but maintain its shape even

when only half-full. It should have a reinforced flap so that crampons can be carried on the outside and it should have exterior straps for an ice axe.

The problem of selecting a large rucksack is far more difficult. Do choose one that is large enough or is expandable.

Framed rucksacks keep the main sack away from your back and this reduces sweating. I will never forget toiling up to the Bétemps Hut in the Swiss Alps on a scorchingly hot July afternoon. We were a party of three and were carrying food and supplies for several days. John was carrying the bread, four long and crusty loaves baked locally in Sion. We arrived at the hut in the late afternoon in a pool of sweat to find that the bread had been packed to the rear of John's rucksack and it was quite sodden with perspiration. None of use could face eating the bread after its baptism by sweat, and we soon went short of supplies.

Different shapes and designs of rucksack suit different people and this is why there is such a handsome selection in the shops. I will list the points you should consider before making your purchase.

1 The rucksack must fit high up on the back and the weight should act downwards, parallel to and as near as possible to the spine, which is the main axis of the body and exceptionally strong. A low-slung and bulky rucksack will exert a torque on the body, throwing the climber off balance and exerting unnecessary strain on the shoulders (*see fig. 39*).

2 The frame of the rucksack should be constructed of light but tough alloy. It needs to be strong because framed rucksacks are rather awkward and bulky, and they take a lot of knocks.

3 The frame should extend above and below the sack so there is plenty of room for attaching bulky items such as sleeping bags and tents.

4 The rucksack should have a wide, padded waist belt with a quick-release buckle in case of emergency. If the bottom of the frame is pulled in towards the body the hips can relieve the shoulders of a good deal of weight.

5 The shoulder straps should be wide and well padded, and all the straps should have easily adjustable buckles. The straps should also be

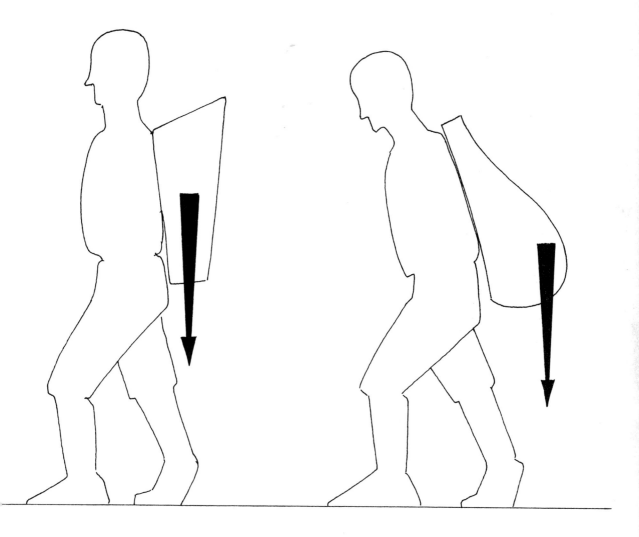

Fig. 39 The correct and incorrect method of carrying a rucksack

long enough for the contents of the pockets to be accessible without having to unthread them from the buckle. This is a godsend when your fingers are numb with cold or when you are wearing mittens. Special straps should be fitted for ice axe attachment.

6 The flap should be large enough to cover and protect large items of equipment, such as a coiled rope or a karrimat, which are tucked under it. The flap should also have provision for the attachment of crampons.

7 Outside pockets are extremely useful. My own rucksack has two on each side plus two map-sized pockets on the front, and they save me having to delve into the sack for oddments.

8 A frameless rucksack has certain definite advantages for the mountaineer. On rock routes where sacks are pulled up on a rope, the framed rucksack will catch on every protruding spike, while the frameless rucksack will not. It is less awkward to carry about and to pack into car boots. But it is important that such a rucksack has an extendable inner section which can be pulled out for carrying big loads. Another advantage of an extendible inner is that in an emergency bivouac the feet can be placed in the sack and the inner pulled right up to the waist. Moreover, once you have set up camp in the mountains, by carrying in food, tent and equipment in your fully extended rucksack, you can use your frameless sack without the extension as a convenient day-sack.

Fig. 40 (a) A frameless expanding rucksack (b) A framed rucksack with padded waist belt

These advantages of the frameless sack may well outweigh the disadvantages of sweating and adaptability for carrying bulky loads. I leave the decision to you (see fig. 40).

Cooking stoves
Cooking in the mountains is not easy and it places special limitations on the suitability of stoves. I shall consider just three different types of stove, each is efficient and each has its own particular merit. These are the butane camping gaz stove, the paraffin Primus stove and the Trangia meths stove (see fig. 41). The solid fuel (meta) stove is not practical because of the weight and expense of the fuel, and the petrol stove is thoroughly dangerous to use. Petrol is highly inflammable and volatile, and it is not

safe to use anywhere near a tent. I know of several accidents which have occurred using petrol stoves and I have had narrow escapes myself.

With the butane gaz stove it is sheer luxury to wake up in the morning and without getting out of your sleeping bag, light the stove, put on the kettle and doze until tea is made. This is possible with the gaz stove because it can be lit immediately, the flame is adjustable and it is clean. For these reasons butane or propane gaz cookers are universally used by car campers and caravaners, but for mountain campers and backpackers there are disadvantages.

Butane boils at the relatively high temperature of $-1°C$, which means that it is not very volatile in cold weather. When camping in winter the gaz cylinders need to be well wrapped up or even taken into your sleeping bag for the night to keep them warm. Propane (boiling point $-42°C$) is much more volatile and can be used efficiently in cold weather but, in order to liquefy the gas, greater pressure is needed and the cylinder walls must be thicker and stronger, and therefore much heavier.

Gaz cylinders are fairly expensive and rather bulky, and it is not always easy to tell the liquid gaz level in the cylinder. Without prior warning, the flame becomes very feeble for the final twenty minutes of a gaz cylinder's life.

The Primus stove has a comforting roar and a characteristic smell of burning paraffin – both closely associated with mountain camping. The heat given out by a well-pressurized Primus is considerably more than either a gaz or a meths stove. Paraffin is cheap and widely available in most countries of the world.

But Primus stoves are fiddly, they have washers that can wear and valves that can be lost, and they can become hopelessly choked by dirty fuel. Primus stoves need meths or solid fuel tablets to prime them, they need prickers to clean their jets and they can be dangerous if mishandled. Paraffin is smelly and can taint food unless it is kept strictly apart, preferably in an outside pocket of the rucksack. A Primus stove of only half-pint capacity is still quite heavy and bulky and even under good conditions it can take five or ten minutes to assemble and light. Wind shields must be taken or constructed since Primus stoves will not function in a draught.

This long list of disadvantages looks daunting but in spite of the care and trouble that must be taken to operate a Primus, there is nothing to beat it for quick and efficient cooking.

The Trangia meths stove is Swedish made but there are several others of similar design made by other manufacturers. The stove comes as an integral part of a complete cooking kit which includes lightweight aluminium saucepans and a carrying handle. The round-bottomed saucepans fit closely over the burner unit so that all the heat from the flame and the hot gases is spread over their entire surface. Excellent all-round heating is obtained and it is rare to burn the porridge or the scrambled egg. The smooth, round surfaces of the cooking pans makes them extremely easy to clean.

Perhaps the main advantage of the Trangia stove is that it can be operated in a draught. Air enters a grid at the base of the stove and helps the hot gases to circulate. The more air that enters the stove the faster the meths burns.

A disc with a hole can be placed over the burner to reduce the flame but fine control of the heat output is not possible. Other disadvantages are the price of methylated spirits, its potential fire risk and the fact that the stove unit, although light, is rather bulky.

Other equipment

A few words of advice about other equipment.

It is difficult to cook well with very thin aluminium pots and pans. I always use a pair of ex-Army mess tins which are robust and just about the right thickness.

Bring a beaker or mug that is plenty big enough, at least of half a pint capacity, and is unbreakable. Aluminium or enamel mugs are not satisfactory because they conduct the heat far too well. Your lips will get burnt or your tea will get cold before you are able to drink it. Polypropylene is a good material for this purpose.

Buy a head torch with a remote battery. This will leave your hands free to put up the tent, hold the map, or do the cooking. Stick a piece of tape or plaster over the switch to ensure that, when packed in your rucksack, it stays in the 'off' position. When you get home from the mountains remove the battery to prevent leakage of corrosive liquids.

A strong polythene bag makes an excellent water container, which can be left at the mouth of the tent.

A small tube of insect repellent could save your sanity on a calm summer's evening when you are camping beside a stream.

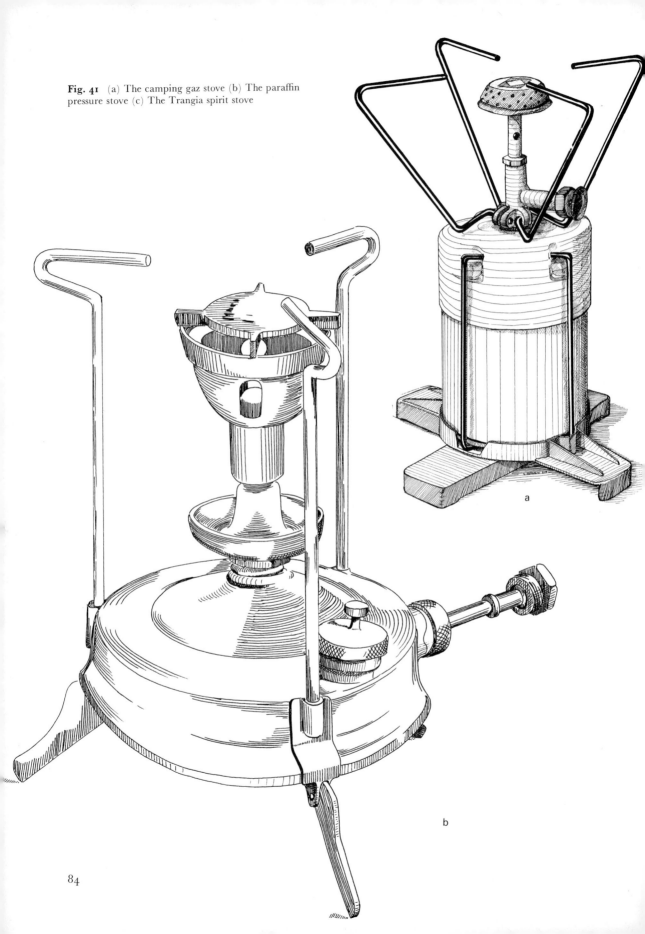

Fig. 41 (a) The camping gaz stove (b) The paraffin pressure stove (c) The Trangia spirit stove

a

b

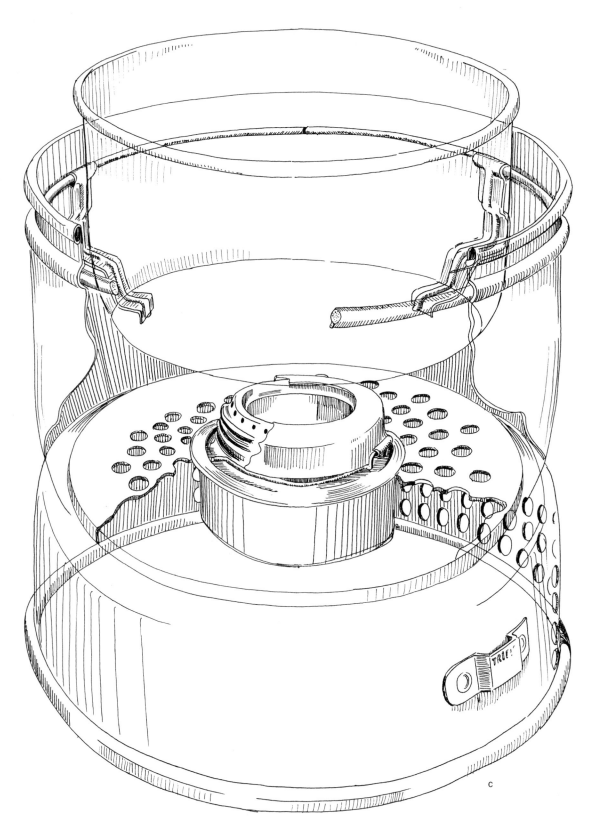

5 Mountain Camping and Backpacking

Mountain camping is a way of life. The camper rubs his nose on the mountains and gets to know their every mood more thoroughly than he could in any other way. The mountain camper is completely independent of the outside world, he is left entirely to his own devices and for me this is one of the main attractions. The pastime of wandering at will through the mountains, carrying tent, equipment and provisions on one's back and camping rough at any suitable site is called backpacking. The backpacker is a self-contained unit.

In modern life we are herded here, there and everywhere. We live strictly controlled lives; forms must be filled in, bills paid, cars driven, queues joined and alarm clocks set for the morning. But the mountain camper can forget the external pressures of the twentieth century and escape to freedom. He can sit back and reflect on life objectively, he can re-adjust his priorities and he has the chance to make decisions for the future. A few days completely away from civilization, camping high in the mountains, is guaranteed to refresh the mind, relax the body and improve one's sanity.

A hankering to return, for a short period of time, to the simple and primitive way of life is inherent in many of us. It is satisfying to feel we can do without centrally heated homes, TVs, and pre-packed foods. We enjoy making blackberry jam and home-made wine, and we like to grow our own vegetables. Living off the land is a challenge which, in extreme cases, leads respectable middle class people to resign from their secure city jobs and to buy ruined crofts in Scotland or Ireland, where they work unbelievably hard just to maintain life at subsistence level.

The mountain camper gets the best of both worlds. He can enjoy the self-righteousness of living the simple life in remote mountain ranges, yet he can still appreciate the comforts of a waterproof tent, a down sleeping bag and a nip of whisky in the evening. The trout which he hauls out of the mountain lake can be grilled for supper over a gaz stove and garnished with accelerated freeze-dried onions, but it is not his staple diet and the catching of it has been motivated by pleasure rather than necessity.

The serious mountaineer must also be a camper because in wild mountain ranges there is no other accommodation available. He must be a knowledgeable and efficient camper too otherwise he will spend so long on the organizational side of camping that he will have no time left for climbing.

On exceptionally long and difficult climbs which take several days or even weeks, the setting up and provisioning of camps play a major role. The expedition to the south-west face of Everest, led by Chris Bonington in 1975, established four camps on the 7500-foot face between the Western Cwm and the summit. Skilled climbers were constantly ferrying loads of food, tents and equipment up to the leading pair to leave them free to concentrate on the actual assault.

Many long climbs in the Alps need intermediate camps and when assistance from others is not possible, the climbers make do with bivvy bags or even snow holes. On the north wall of the Eiger, for example, there are no ledges sufficiently wide for tents to be erected and bivouacs are essential. Without the protection of a tent you become extremely vulnerable to bad weather and this is one of the prime reasons for the horrific accident rate on the Eiger.

Detailed consideration of bivouacs and snow holes, except for use in emergencies, is beyond the scope of this book and I shall concentrate on camping in its normal sense.

30 Away from it all. Climbing in Antarctica. (Photograph by I. Sykes)

In the early days, when my life-long love of the Highlands of Scotland was beginning to blossom, I was fascinated by the huge tract of mountainous country encompassing the three great glens of the western Highlands. Glens Affric, Cannich and Strathfarrar sit astride the watershed of Scotland and none of them have been far penetrated by motor roads. It was obvious that a backpacking expedition would be necessary to reach the innermost sanctuaries of the mountains. My friend Alan shared my enthusiasm for the Highlands and we planned a backpacking walk round the ridges overlooking Loch Mullardoch in Glen Cannich. We were young and inexperienced and it was very much a pioneering expedition; it gave us our first taste of high mountain camping in winter, for it was mid-March and bitterly cold.

Our equipment was adequate but heavy and we toiled up the snow-covered ridges, sometimes wearing crampons and sometimes cutting steps, bowed down by our rucksacks. The weather was mainly poor with mist and snow flurries but the occasional gap in the cloud cover showed up the Scottish peaks to their best advantage. From Mam Soul (3862 feet) shafts of sunlight played on the surface of Loch Affric far below and the sight of the old pine forest at the edge of the loch made a welcome change from our white world. Arctic hares, ptarmigan and snow bunting abounded and a dark brown fox emerged from the boulders at the summit of Sgurr nan Ceathreamhnan. Alan wore an old Harris Tweed jacket for most of the trip. He had been reading classic accounts of mountaineering at the turn of the century and was determined that what had been good enough for the old timers should be good enough for him.

At nightfall we erected the tent on the nearest flat platform we could find, settled down in our sleeping bags and cooked by candlelight. Of course, having the tent with us always was extremely comforting, particularly when we lost our way or the weather deteriorated. Our boots froze solid at night and the eggs had to be prized out of their shells but all was forgotten in the evening when we lay smoking our pipes, sipping whisky and calculating the day's tally of Munros.

This five-day backpacking expedition was hugely enjoyable and was the first of many. March and April make ideal months for mountain camping, you don't get too hot under the weight of a heavy rucksack, there are no midges and even rounded and rather featureless hills become challenging objectives under a coating of snow and ice.

The feelings of security and well-being which are so important in mountain camping are only possible if you have complete confidence in your equipment. Reliable, well-proven equipment is the key to successful mountain camping. I would much rather carry a few extra pounds in my rucksack, and not have to worry about the ability of the tent to survive a storm, than to lie shivering in my sleeping bag anxiously awaiting each buffet of wind roaring up the glen and shaking the tent. When you have been battling all day against the elements, you need proper protection from them at night.

Packing your rucksack

Let us assume that you have gathered together the correct equipment and are planning, with a friend, a three-night backpacking expedition

over the mountains in early spring. Here is a list of essentials that you should have with you. Running your eyes down a checklist may save you the embarrassment and discomfort of leaving behind a vital item.

Individual	*Shared*
Rucksack lined with polythene bag	Tent and fly-sheet
Ice axe	Stove, fuel and funnel
Crampons	Candles
Sleeping bag	Matches
Karrimat	Billy cans and kettle
Spare jersey	Pan scourer
Balaclava helmet	First-aid kit
Knife, fork, spoon	Absorbent toilet paper
Plate and mug	Tin opener
Torch	Water bottle
Gloves	Flask of whisky
Spare pair of socks	20 m. of 9-mm. rope
Anorak	
Waterproof over-trousers	
Long Johns or pyjamas	
Note book and pencil	
Paperback reading book	
Toothbrush	
Camera	
Map, compass and whistle	
Map case or transparent polythene bag	
Money	

You will notice that very little spare clothing is allowed for on my list. If you have really good waterproofs and provided that you stay put or camp early in the face of torrential rain, you should not get very wet. Of course your socks will get wet and your shirt is bound to get damp, but if you wear them inside your sleeping bag at night they will have dried out by morning.

The rope is more of a safeguard and is unlikely to be in constant use. You may need it for a short abseil or for security whilst negotiating an exposed scramble. In wet weather you may need it for river crossings and in stormy weather it can act as an extra main guy rope for the tent.

Absorbent toilet paper is very useful when your partner spills the pan of soup inside the tent. It can also be used for wiping cutlery and making a cursory clean up when it is too wet or too cold to leave the tent. A pan scourer weighs practically nothing and saves hours of scrubbing with grass or heather. Try to acquire an ultra-lightweight tin opener (*as in fig. 42*); they are supplied in Army compo-ration packs and they are most efficient. Attach a piece of coloured wool or string to the tin opener and you will be less likely to lose it. Although it is quite possible to open a tin with an ice axe, it is a messy and time-consuming operation.

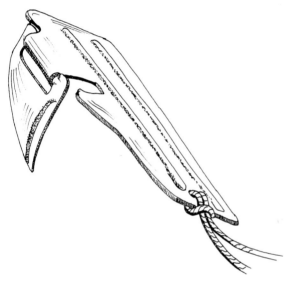

Fig. 42 Lightweight can opener

Perhaps you will think it extravagant of me to include reading matter and a flask of whisky on the list, but it is important to be able to relax at the end of a long day in the mountains and a nip of whisky followed by a chapter or two of a good book, whilst snuggled in your sleeping bag, is a recipe for a good night's sleep.

It is very tempting to pack in all sorts of extra items which would be useful but are not essential. I am thinking of toothpaste, towel, razor, gym shoes etc., but this is a mountaineering expedition with overnight camps, not a camping holiday where the tent is pitched adjacent to your car. It pays many times over to be utterly ruthless in the selection of your food and equipment. You will derive

far greater benefit from the luxury of a light rucksack than from the extra items themselves. As a guide, aim for a maximum weight limit of 35 pounds. A pack of much more than this weight can turn a backpacking expedition into a nightmare, but a moderate and well-designed rucksack will soon become part of you and you will hardly notice the burden.

If, however, you plan to walk into a base in the mountains where you will camp for a week at just one particular site, then your equipment list would look rather different. You will be able to manage a very heavy rucksack for a single day's walk through the valley and so you can include many luxury items of your choice. I would take some fresh vegetables, tinned food, a thermos flask, an extra stove, a bottle of wine and a duvet jacket.

A few years ago I took a party of boys on a climbing expedition to the spectacular peaks of the Lyngen Peninsula in Arctic Norway. One of the boys had not heeded my plea to leave behind all unnecessary items of equipment and he insisted on taking a battery razor, after-shave lotion, suede shoes, overcoat, chocolates, fishing tackle, an inflatable air bed and many other luxury goods. As we left the road end for the three-hour walk to base camp he was carrying an 80-pound rucksack, an Army kit bag slung over one shoulder and a bulging zip bag in each hand. The going was hard, through scrub and over boulder fields, it was extremely hot and the mosquitoes were buzzing round our heads. Quite soon our overloaded friend jettisoned the kit bag and zip bags, and hid them under a bush. Having successfully reached base camp, he erected his tent and returned to the lower slopes where he hunted for his cache of luxury goods. It took him two days and an organized sweep search to find the cache but the lesson had got home.

When you have assembled all the food and equipment in a large pile on the floor it may look rather daunting but it should all pack away neatly into a well-designed rucksack. I have yet to find a really waterproof rucksack so I recommend that you line yours with a large polythene bag. Any farmer will give you an old blue fertilizer bag; wash it out and you will find that it is just about the right size as well as being tough enough for the job. Dustbin liners are also the right size but they are too thin and they tear easily. A number of thinner and smaller polythene bags will come in useful for protecting items such as your camera, film, books and matches.

Pack your rucksack sensibly to make it as comfortable as possible. Keep hard, angular objects such as tins and stoves well away from the back of the rucksack. A sleeping bag or unrolled karrimat, if it is narrow enough, can serve as a useful pad when it is inserted down the back of the rucksack. Of course if you are using a pack frame, the sack is kept well away from your back and there is no problem. Don't bury items that you might need on the walk deep in your rucksack. Keep your anorak, over-trousers, gloves, balaclava and spare jersey near the top and keep your lunch, the map and compass and camera in the side pockets. If you are cooking on a paraffin or meths stove keep the fuel well away from the food and the rope (organic solvents can quickly ruin a rope); if possible put it in a side pocket. Bulky items such as the tent, the fly-sheet and rolled-up karrimats will fit under the main flap or, if this is impossible, they can be strapped on to the top.

The rucksack must be well balanced. This is particularly important if you are rock scrambling, traversing a narrow ridge or boulder hopping across a river where a sudden lurch could cause you to lose your footing. Make sure the rucksack waist band is secured.

Establishing camp

Although it is possible to camp almost anywhere in the mountains, you will probably have planned the day's walk with a camp site in mind. As a highly mobile camper you will have a wide choice and beautiful sites abound. You may choose to camp beside a remote lake, a tumbling stream, in an amphitheatre of cliffs, on a grassy ledge overlooking a valley or the sea. When you are deciding on the exact location for your tent remember these points:

1 You can never be sure, particularly in the mountains, that the weather will stay fine, so you must consider pitching the tent on a site that is sheltered from the prevailing wind. In the lee of a ridge, a large boulder or a bluff of rock will make all the difference if a squall blows up.

2 Make sure that running water is nearby. Mountain stream water is almost always pure and fit for drinking so don't worry about health hazards. But don't pitch the tent on the stream bank because the water level can rise incredibly quickly and a 'flash flood', which is a severe local storm, could wash you away. Bear in mind that rainfall in excess of eight inches a day is not unknown in the mountains of Britain. For the same reason try to avoid camping in a hollow or near a runnel, however dry the ground seems to be when you arrive.

3 If the mountains are snow covered it is always worth descending below the snowline to camp near running water. Melting snow for cooking and drinking purposes is a lengthy process and it uses much fuel. To make a pint of boiling water from snow takes twice as much heat as starting from cold water. In addition a very large volume of snow makes only a very small volume of water.

4 Spend a moment or two looking for a patch of ground that is firm and well drained. Brush away any sharp stones or pieces of heather root which might puncture the groundsheet.

When you are planning the day's walk from the map remember that unless you are exceptionally fit, you must modify Naismith's Rule (*see page 14*) to take into account your pack. Allow plenty of time for choosing the camp site and never stint on efficiency while erecting the tent. Arriving at a camp site, perhaps in driving rain, weary from the day's mountaineering and longing above all for a warm sleeping bag and a large brew, it is all too easy to put up the tent haphazardly without thought of what the night may bring. I have been guilty of this myself on many occasions, almost always with dire results.

Put the pegs in firmly and at the correct angle, (*as in fig. 43*), place stones on the valance, tighten the guys and, however fine the evening, erect the fly-sheet. Hook the guy ropes into the notches on the runners to prevent them slipping. If the ground is too frozen or rocky to take pegs you must find some large boulders and tie the guy ropes to them. On the other hand if the ground is too sodden and soft to grip the pegs you could use the ice axes to anchor the main guys, failing that, roll heavy stones on top of the pegs.

31 Base camp, Greenland. (Photograph by D. Fordham)

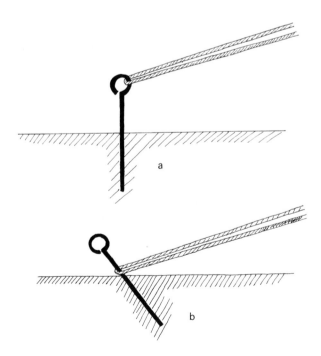

Fig. 43 Inserting a tent peg (a) Incorrect (b) Correct

Re-erecting a half-collapsed tent in a storm and in pitch blackness is a hideous experience and one which can usually be avoided. However, if you do wake to a flapping fly-sheet or a drip from the roof, get up, go outside and do something about it. Don't bury your head in your pillow and hope the trouble will go away.

I once camped beside the tiny Loch Toll an Lochain (2000 feet) under the great cliffs of An Teallach in Ross-shire. A site that, for grandeur, cannot be surpassed in Britain. It was early November and on the first night a terrible gale blew in from the west. My companions in the tent next door were a recently engaged couple and at 3.00 a.m. the main front pole of their tent snapped clean off, although it was made of alloy. Heroically my friend, Mike, held up the stump of the pole for three hours to provide partial protection, but the rain seeped in and sloshed about on the floor of the tent. Mike's fianceé slept through the entire night quite unaware of the drama being played out beside her. By first light Mike was suffering mild exposure and came into my tent for tea and hot porridge. We rolled up the sodden tents and fled to Shenavall bothy three miles away.

Camp cooking

As the day wears on and you carry your pack over the mountains and down into the valleys your thoughts are certain to turn to the evening meal and the delicacies that you have stowed away in your rucksack. For this reason alone the choice of food is very important. Likes and dislikes are very personal and the variety of convenience foods which are now available in the shops is very wide but here are some of the factors which you should consider before making your final selection.

1 Bring plenty of food. When you are engaged in strenuous mountaineering pursuits, and backpacking over the hills is very strenuous, you will get extremely hungry and you need to be supplied with about 4000 calories a day. If you consume less you are much more likely to feel faint and weak, and to suffer from cold and even hypothermia.

2 The food that you take with you must be palatable. This will encourage you to eat well and it will add greatly to the pleasure of living in the mountains. It has been recognized for many years that good food on expeditions boosts morale. As early as 1922 General Bruce's Everest expedition gorged themselves on quails in truffles, crystallized ginger, tinned hams and herrings and all this at over 25,000 feet. Tasty morsels are the best cure for lethargy and lack of appetite.

3 Although very lightweight dried food is available, don't make your selection solely on the weight factor. Curried beef powder and string beans are admirably light but become very boring after a few days. If you do decide to bring some rather heavy foods such as eggs, sausages, baked beans or fruit cake, eat them early on during the expedition so you won't have to carry them far. Go for variety and aim for at least one treat every night.

4 Try to buy food that can be simply and quickly cooked. When you have erected the tent you will want to eat promptly, so don't buy meals which need simmering or steaming for hours. Christmas pudding is delicious but it has to be steamed for four hours and thus is quite impractical. Complete meals sealed in aluminium foil sachets are excellent and they need only heating in boiling water for five minutes. When the sachets have been removed from the pan the hot water can be used for soup or tea. Quick meals save fuel as well as temper and the shorter the time that the mess tin is balanced on the stove the less likely it is to be knocked over.

5 Keep the menu as simple as possible. If you have only one stove and a limited number of mess tins it is impossible to cook a meal of many separate dishes. Stew or paella are ideal because everything is thrown together in the one pot. Porridge is popular with many campers but I find that it lies very heavy on the stomach during the day and washing up the dirty pots in ice-cold water is difficult, unpleasant and time-consuming. Muesli is just as nutritious, far cleaner and needs little preparation. If you mix dried milk powder into the muesli before leaving home you need only add cold water and stir.

6 Bring lots of tea bags and lots of soup powder. Your first priority at camp is to replace the fluid lost through your exertions of the day and the soft water of mountain streams is flat and not very good for drinking without extra flavouring. If you add some lemonade crystals to your water bottle you will be more inclined to drink during the day.

At altitude, where the air is often very dry, the body loses water through the pores at a high rate and in the Himalayas you should drink a minimum of eight pints a day. Dehydration can bring fatigue and lassitude to the unwary. Although I don't usually take sugar in my tea I do find that after a day's backpacking a mug of sweet tea revives me quicker than anything. If you are tired at the end of the day, and are not pressed for time, it is a good idea to make a brew before doing anything else, even before putting up the tent.

For a backpacking expedition to the mountains I make up my menus from the following list of items. The choice is, of course, personal but it may give you some ideas to help with your own selection.

Breakfasts: Muesli, dried milk powder, sugar, tea bags, plain biscuits, margarine, jam, pre-packed bacon, dried egg powder.

Lunches: Lemonade powder, tubed cheese, sweet biscuits, chocolate, salted peanuts, raisins, sardines, apples, smoked sausage.

Suppers: One cup instant soups, AFD meals and vegetables, sachet meals, dried potato powder, dried onions, salt, instant whips and desserts, dried apple rings, cheese and biscuits.

Treats: Tinned mandarin oranges, anchovies, chutney, tin of condensed milk, jar of honey.

Before you start cooking it is as well to get the tent and your belongings properly organized. Small lightweight tents don't have much room for two adults unless everything is stowed away. Your tent will probably have a most useful space or porch between the inner tent and the front fly-sheet extension. Some fly-sheets zip right down to the ground making a porch that is completely sheltered from wind and rain. This porch should be used for cooking so that any spills or mess can be kept off the groundsheet of the inner tent. Also it reduces the risk of fire. If your porch is open to the elements you must bring or construct an efficient wind shield. Stoves are difficult to light in a draught and the heat loss by convection is considerable, thereby wasting precious fuel. For the same reason you should always cover mess tins when heating them on the stove. I find it worthwhile to bring a lightweight aluminium kettle for boiling water, the extra weight is more than cancelled out by the resultant saving of fuel.

Your food should be carefully packed in screw-top aluminium or polythene jars or in tough polythene bags. These jars together with tins, spare gas cylinders, plates and cooking pots can be tucked away at the side of the tent between the inner and the fly-sheet. Strong waterproof packaging for food is essential. A burst bag of powdered milk or a meal sachet will make a terrible mess in your rucksack.

Unpack the sleeping bags from their waterproof sacks so that the down has time to fluff out and completely fill the box compartments. You can use the waterproof sacks to cover your rucksacks which can then be left outside the tent. Framed rucksacks are awkward and take up vital space inside the tent. The thin nylon bags which contained your sleeping bags make excellent 'stuff sacks' for oddments.

Insist that boots are removed before entering the tent. Leave them in the porch where they can be useful for holding mugs of tea and cutlery.

Stand the stove on a large flat stone and check that it is quite firm before you light it. If you are using a Primus (pressure) stove be especially circumspect and always ensure that the burner has been sufficiently heated by the solid fuel tablets before you start pumping the paraffin through. Pressure stoves can become flame throwers unless they are expertly handled.

These points that I have made about camp organization are flexible. If you arrive at the camp site in bad weather, utterly worn out and frozen to the marrow, you must take immediate action. Erect the tent quickly, fill several receptacles with water and pile into the inner tent as quickly as possible, boots, rucksack and all, and fasten the entrance flap. Light the stove and put on the kettle for tea, the temperature will rise rapidly and you will soon be warm and snug, and feeling human again. This is where the safety aspect of backpacking comes in. In a very short time you have changed a potentially dangerous situation, resulting from cold and exhaustion, into one of security and snugness.

Before you settle down for the night think what you will need for breakfast in the morning and make a few preparations. Fill the water bottle and kettle and check the level of paraffin in the Primus. It should be possible for you to make breakfast without having to leave your sleeping bag. An early start in the morning increases your options when it comes to deciding the route and it widens the safety margin. After the supper dishes have been cleared away you can retire to your sleeping bag with a last brew. Light the candle and read a chapter of your book or write up your log. You wouldn't change your perch in the mountains for a five star hotel, would you?

Packing up

This is a simple procedure unless it is wet, in which case remain in the tent until you have packed your rucksack. Dispense with the washing up. Put on waterproofs and dismantle the tent. Shake the surplus droplets off the fly-sheet before you fold it up and deal with the inner tent as quickly as possible before it too becomes wet. Cotton tents become very much heavier when they are wet but nylon tents do not soak up water to anything like the same

33 An uncomfortable mountain camp. Changabang.
(Photograph by J. Tasker)

degree. Flatten tins and take all your rubbish
back with you in a polythene bag which can
go in an outside pocket of the rucksack. Never
dump rubbish, because even after years of
burial plastics and aluminium do not degrade.

Mountain bothies and shelters

During your expeditions through the
mountains you will sometimes come upon
mountain shelters. In the remote valleys and
glens there may be stone-built cottages and on
some of the high plateaus and cols there may
be emergency refuges. Most of the cottages, or
bothies as they are called in Scotland, are now
ruined, for they were built during the
nineteenth century to house shepherds and
gillies, a dying breed of estate worker. Life in
these isolated homesteads was very hard and
when the tenants left, the landlords would
remove the roofs of the houses so that they
would not be liable for taxes.

In 1965 a voluntary organization called The
Mountain Bothies Association was set up with
the object of renovating certain bothies. The
MBA has done a magnificent job and,
although working on a very small budget, they
have re-roofed and re-floored many bothies
often manhauling timber, roofing sheets and
cement over miles of rough country. The
renovated bothies are primitive but weatherproof and are open to all comers, free of
charge, at all times.

After a few days' backpacking it makes a
pleasant change to spend the night in a bothy.
There is room to stretch out, there may be a
table and chairs and almost certainly there will
be a fireplace. Bothies can be cold and damp
unless a good fire is roaring up the chimney
but fuel can sometimes prove hard to find.
Drift wood can often be collected from the
banks of lakes and streams and even peat bogs
can provide 'bog wood', the ancient whitened
roots of trees from the old Caledonian forest
which covered the Highlands with oak, hazel,
birch and Scots pine. Dry your clothes, air

your sleeping bag and toast your toes in front
of the fire but always remember to leave a
plentiful supply of dry wood in the bothy for
the next user.

Bad bothies should be left well alone. These
have leaking roofs, muddy earth floors and
draughty windows, and you are better off in
the tent. Rats can be a problem in some
bothies, they carry disease and they do not
make ideal sleeping companions. A friend of
mine woke up one night in a remote bothy to
find a rat inside his sleeping bag. If you suspect
rats, place all your food in bags and hang them
up from the rafters, otherwise these voracious
rodents will be sure to devour it.

Never plan to spend the night in emergency
shelters. They should be used only as a last
resort and many mountain rescue team leaders
consider they cause more accidents than they
save. In bad conditions these low igloo-type
buildings are hard to find and when deep snow
lies on the hills they may be completely buried.
It is often better to use the time, which you
might spend looking for the emergency shelter,
in making a speedy descent to lower ground.
For this reason many shelters have now been
dismantled, although on some maps they are
still shown as being in position.

6 Navigation

An ability to navigate quickly and accurately is the single most important skill that must be acquired by the mountaineer. He must know exactly where he is at all times and, in misty weather or darkness, he must know how to plot a course on the map and follow it in the mountains by the use of a compass. Mists, clouds and fogs tend to hang about in mountainous areas and if you turn back for home every time the visibility gets poor you will not achieve many summits.

Maps

Maps contain a wealth of vital information and there are maps for everybody. Motorists, meteorologists, geologists and historians are a few of the specialists that are catered for by the cartographers. The mountaineer and hill walker needs to have the best available information on topographical features and Ordnance Survey maps are the most suitable for this purpose. Sit down for five minutes and carefully scrutinize an OS map. These remarkable documents contain an astonishing assortment of facts: roads, footpaths, rights of way, cliffs, marshes, lakes, streams, car parks and a host of other fascinating details.

The one inch to one mile (1:63,360) scale OS maps are rapidly being phased out and replaced by the larger scale 1:50,000 metric series where 2 centimetres on the map equals 1 kilometre on the ground. In addition the OS produce Outdoor Leisure maps of 1:25,000 scale for certain popular areas of hill country. These excellent maps have a large enough scale (roughly $2\frac{1}{2}$ inches to the mile) for all the footpaths, sheep pens and natural landmarks to be shown.

The British OS maps have a grid of 1-kilometre squares superimposed on the map detail. The distance between the grid lines

represents 1 kilometre on the ground and the vertical lines point north. Numbers are allocated to the grid lines to provide a reference system for any point on the map and these grid numbers are exactly the same whatever scale of map you are using. By convention the eastings are written down first followed by the northings, three figures for each making up a six-figure map reference. An example is given in fig. 44. The six-figure map reference of point 'A' is 428771. For accuracy in working out exact references the calibrations on the side of your compass can be used. Point 'A' will be accurate to about 50 metres on the ground.

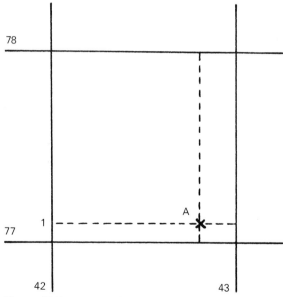

Fig. 44 Taking a map reference

Mixing up the northings and eastings of a map reference can lead to disaster and so here is an aid to memory. 'When you enter a house you walk across the hall and then climb the stairs.' Likewise on a map you record the horizontal grid reference (easting) before the vertical one (northing). As a last resort the convention for references is explained in the key on every OS map.

But mountaineers need more than just large-scale maps to help them with their navigation, they need accurate contour lines to determine heights and angles of slopes. Contour lines connect points of the same height above sea level and the interpretation of them comes only after careful study. The one inch to the mile OS maps have contour lines drawn at intervals of 50 feet, the metric maps at intervals of 10 metres. Every fifth contour line is printed in heavier type with the height that it represents written in at regular intervals. When planning a route it is necessary to count the contour lines which will be crossed in order to obtain an estimate of the height to be gained and lost.

Steep slopes are indicated by closely spaced contour lines and plateaus by either widely spaced lines or the absence of lines altogether. In misty weather when you are descending a steep and possibly tricky slope, you will need to know what lies ahead. If you are on a concave slope the angle will ease but if it is convex the angle will increase and you may be forced to retreat. When you are fumbling with the map in a high wind and poor visibility, it is easy to misinterpret the features. Fig. 45 gives the map

representation of some common features which are not always fully understood.

Certain types of OS maps have purple shading to bring out the shape of the ridges. The shading represents the shadow which would be thrown by the mountain outlines when the sun sets in the north-west. Other maps (but not those made by the OS) have different colours for different heights so that areas of high ground can easily be recognized. This technique is known as layering.

The map is the mountaineer's constant companion and with practice you will be able to read a map as easily as a book. Keep the

Fig. 45 The interpretation of contours

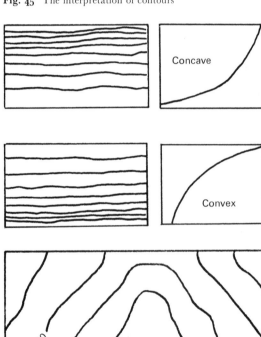

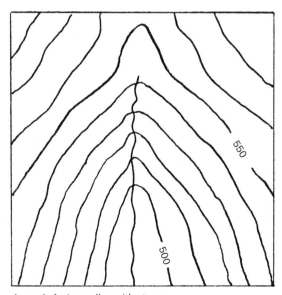

A south-facing valley with stream

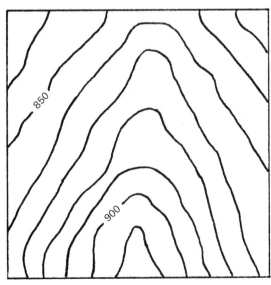

A mountain spur descending to the north

map handy for constant reference and look after it well. You may find it useful to cover the map with self-adhesive transparent film but in any case it should always be kept clean and dry in a polythene bag. If you are using a particular section of the map which is near the middle of the sheet you can pencil in the grid reference numbers. You can now fold the map to display the required area and all the information you need will be there in front of you.

The magnetic variation

The meridians that join the true north and south poles are called lines of longitude and these lines point to true north. The grid lines on the map point to grid north which, for our purposes, can be taken as identical to true north.

A compass needle points to magnetic north. The magnetic north pole is not stationary, neither does it coincide with grid north, and the difference between the two is known as the magnetic variation. At the time of writing the magnetic variation in Great Britain is about 8° west of grid north and it is decreasing at a rate of 1° every ten years (*see fig. 46*). Since the variation also changes from place to place, the grid-magnetic variation corresponding to a particular area is always printed at the bottom of the map.

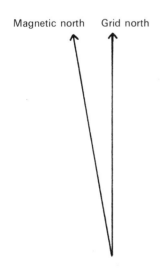

Fig. 46 Magnetic variation

It is most important to appreciate the significance of the magnetic variation and to understand that the compass needle does not point in the same direction as the grid lines on the map. Several years ago I was exploring the Myrdals Jokull ice cap in south-west Iceland with a party of schoolboys, and as we slowly climbed the vast grey ice sheet we became enveloped in a thick and clinging mist. The crevasses in the ice became covered by wet snow and I considered it prudent to retreat on a compass bearing. To my surprise we did not arrive back at our starting point but at an area of treacherous quick-sands which caused us much trouble and alarm. Later that night I realized that my mistake lay in taking the magnetic variation as 8° and not as 30°, which was the correct figure for that part of Iceland.

The compass

The type of compass which is most frequently used by mountaineers is that which combines conventional magnetic compass with protractor. This type of compass is known as a Silva compass named after the company which first designed it (*see fig. 47*). The compass housing is rotatable and it is set on a transparent (perspex) base. The magnetized side of the needle which points north is usually painted red with a dab of luminous paint on the tip. The 360° of a circle are printed on the outside edge of the housing, while the inside is filled with oil or alcohol to dampen the swing of the needle. For calculating distances and for accurate map reference determinations the edges of the base plate are sometimes calibrated in inches and millimetres.

The Silva compass is light and easy to use, and it is quite accurate enough for most work including international orienteering events. It is used for four main purposes: setting the map, taking a bearing, walking on a bearing and determining position by taking back bearings.

Setting the map

In clear weather, features on the landscape can be easily identified by setting the map. This means that when the map is held flat the orientation is such that the actual landscape features are in line with those printed on the

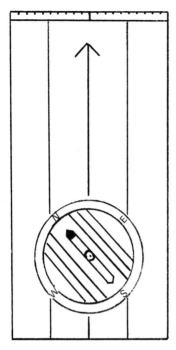

Fig. 47 The Silva compass

there are 360° in a complete circle. East corresponds to 90° (from north), south to 180° and so on. The advantage in taking a compass bearing in degrees is that far greater accuracy can be obtained. Thus, to quote a bearing of 272° is much better than saying just north of west (*see fig. 48*).

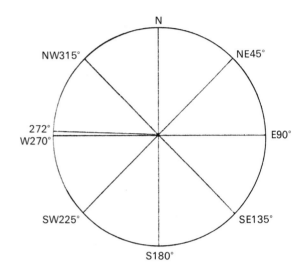

Fig. 48 The compass points

map. When studying a map that has been set, the map appears as a scaled down version of the ground itself. Features can now be recognized and this will help you to work out your location if it is in doubt.

Place the map flat on the ground with the compass on top. Rotate the compass housing until it is set at a bearing of 8° (or the appropriate magnetic variation). Line up the edge of the compass with a north-pointing grid line and then rotate compass and map together until the red needle is aligned with the 'N' mark on the dial. The map is now set. Don't worry if the writing on the map appears upside down, this is bound to happen if you are facing south.

If you know your exact position and can recognize the features on the ground you need not use the compass; just line up these features with those printed on the map. The top of the map should now point north and, as before, the map is set.

Taking a bearing

The points on a compass are measured in degrees and, as you learn in school geometry,

Bearings can be useful in two ways. Firstly, you may get a few minutes' warning of an approaching storm or fog bank and you can quickly take a bearing on your next objective before the landscape is blotted out. Armed with this bearing you can now walk on, confident in the knowledge that you are going in the right direction. To obtain the bearing you should line up the main axis of the compass, as indicated by the direction of travel arrow, with your next objective. Then rotate the compass housing until the red pointer coincides with the 'N' arrow of the surround and read off the correct bearing from the point marked by the direction of travel arrow.

Secondly, a bearing taken from the map can easily be translated into a magnetic bearing for compass use. In this way, provided you know your exact location on the map, you can proceed in the correct direction towards any other point of your choice.

As an example, suppose you are standing on the summit of Beinn Ghlas in thick mist and you want to reach the summit of Ben Lawers.

First of all use the compass as a protractor to find the correct bearing from the map. Line up the edge of the compass with the summits of the two mountains and twist the circular surround until the lines etched on the base of the compass are aligned with the north-south grid lines of the map. The bearing in degrees can now be read off the dial where it meets the direction of travel arrow (*as in fig. 49*). The correct bearing is 43° and note that throughout this operation so far it does not matter in which direction the compass needle is pointing. You can now fold up the map and having added 8° to the map bearing, you can march on a magnetic compass bearing of 51° which will lead you to the summit cairn of Ben Lawers.

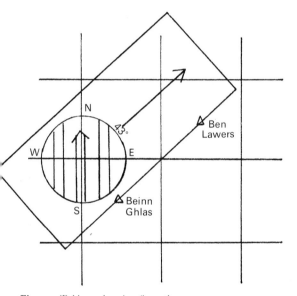

Fig. 49 Taking a bearing from the map

It is vital that you do not confuse the necessary correction due to the magnetic variation. If you were to subtract the variation from the grid bearing instead of adding it, your direction of travel, as indicated by the compass, would be out by 16°. Two aids to memory are:
—'Variation west magnetic best. Variation east magnetic least.' This means that when the magnetic variation is to the west of north the magnetic bearing is always greater than the grid bearing. But when the variation is east of

north the magnetic bearing is less than the grid bearing.
—'The landscape is bigger than the map.' Therefore the bearing for the landscape (magnetic) should be bigger than that for the map (grid).

Walking on a bearing

Let us assume that you have used your map and compass to obtain the correct grid bearing of your objective and you have corrected for magnetic variation. Now you must follow this bearing as accurately as possible.

Rotate the circular dial of your compass until the bearing is set to the required figure (51° for Ben Lawers). Now move the entire compass until the red needle points to the 'N' point on the dial. Walk in the direction of the main arrow to your destination (*see fig. 50*).

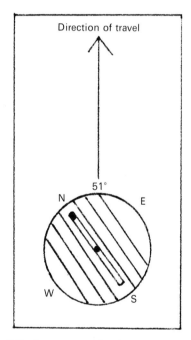

Fig. 50 Following a compass bearing

In complex mountain country it is not always easy to follow the relatively short arrow indicating the direction of travel. You will find it easier to sight along the arrow and pick a landmark about 50 metres ahead of you in the correct direction. When you have reached that spot use the compass again and continue the sighting procedure step-wise until you have arrived at your destination.

In thick mist or white-out conditions, when it is impossible to see landmarks even at close range, you can use other members of your party to help. Line them up at intervals of about 2 metres, or until the furthest man is at the limit of your visibility, and shout commands to get the line into exactly the correct direction as indicated by the compass. Walk to the front of the line and then repeat the procedure. This is a tedious and time-consuming method of advance but it is vitally important to ensure as far as possible that the correct bearing is being followed.

The errors introduced by quite small deviations from the correct bearing are alarming. For example if you stray off bearing by an average of $5°$ you will end up 87 metres away from your intended objective after walking 1 kilometre and 435 metres away after 5 kilometres. To be within 5 metres of the objective after 1 kilometre your accuracy must be as good as $\frac{1}{4}°$, clearly this is impossible. From a safety point of view this means that in conditions of very poor visibility you are most unlikely to find a small tent or shelter which is situated on an area of open ground with no other recognizable features nearby. When you are traversing sloping ground and when there is a strong side wind tending to push you off course, you will be doing well to keep within $5°$ of the correct bearing.

Determining position

If you are unsure of your position on the map but can identify two or more visible features of the landscape, it is possible, by means of resectioning, to determine your exact position. Basically the technique involves finding the bearings of the known features and drawing in their back bearings on the map. Your true position is then at the intersection of the back bearings. Four procedures are necessary:

1 Take bearings on two or more known landmarks which should be as widely spaced as possible.

34 Taking a compass bearing in the Lyngen Range, Arctic Norway.

2 Subtract the magnetic variation to obtain the corresponding grid bearings.

3 To obtain the back bearings subtract 180° from the grid bearings or, if this is impossible because the grid bearing is less than 180°, add 180°.

4 From the landmarks on the map and using the compass as a protractor, draw lines in the direction of the corresponding back bearings. Your present position will be at the intersection of the lines.

As an example, let us return to Perthshire and assume that we can identify the three separate peaks of Ben Lawers, Beinn Ghlas and Meall a'Choire Leith but we are not sure of our exact position. As in fig. 51, we take sightings of these three peaks to obtain:

Fig. 51 Taking back bearings

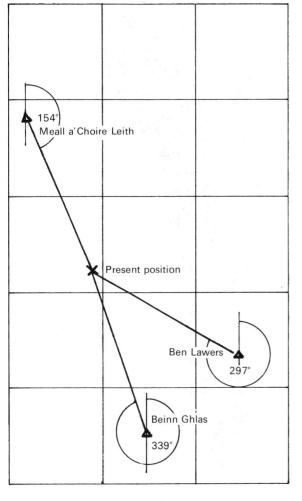

	Ben Lawers	Beinn Ghlas	Meall a'Choire Leith
Compass bearings	125°	167°	342°
Grid bearings	117°	159°	334°
Back bearing	297°	339°	154°

As you can see from the diagram the back bearings intersect at our present position.

Estimating distance

We have seen how difficult it can be to walk accurately on a compass bearing in bad weather and how even small errors can put route finding badly awry. But if we are trying to locate a spot position in poor visibility we need to estimate distance as well as direction. It is here that experience is all important. Walking speed is affected by terrain, snow condition, gradient, wind, fatigue and the load you are carrying, and for this reason Naismith's Rule, which is discussed on page 14, is only the roughest of guides. The experienced walker develops a second sense of speed and distance, and he can estimate the ground he has covered under varying conditions by use of his watch. From countless mountain days in all conditions he knows his speed up hill, down hill and across plateaux and this information stands him in good stead when the clouds are down.

I find that when climbing in Scotland the slope of the ground, the nature of the rocks, vegetation, moss and lichens, wind and temperature enable me to estimate my height and my present whereabouts even in poor visibility.

When navigating in bad conditions it is sometimes worthwhile to aim off deliberately. It may be that your next summit is at the western edge of a line of cliffs. If you aim directly for the summit you could miss it, but if you plot your course a few degrees east of the summit you should easily recognize the cliff edge when you come to it and you can then follow it west until the summit is reached.

Remember that in bad visibility it is extremely important to know exactly where you are although you may not be exactly where you want to be. For this reason you should navigate from landmark to landmark, keeping each leg as short as possible.

Navigation hints

1 Trust the compass. It is very easy to become completely disorientated in bad weather without realizing it. Don't rely on instinct, you are almost certain to be wrong.

2 The compass needle is attracted to metal objects. When taking a bearing it is most important to keep the ice axe, rucksack buckles, karabiners and zip fasteners well away from the compass. Before setting out check the guide book to find if there are any magnetic rocks in your area. In some mountain ranges, the Cuillin of Skye for example, the compass is almost useless as an aid to navigation.

3 In conditions of high wind, rain and snow it is very difficult to manhandle the map, let alone take an accurate bearing. You will find it simpler to do your homework before setting out in the shelter of your hut or tent. Write down on a piece of card the principal landmarks of the day's walk, together with the corresponding compass bearings. Keep the card in an anorak pocket or inside your glove so you can quickly and simply refer to it.

4 When you first unfold a map, check the date of its last revision. If you are relying on the magnetic variation as printed on the map the date will be important so that you can calculate the present variation. The date is also important when considering recent man-made changes to the natural scene such as hydro-electric schemes, new roads and forestry plantations.

5 For night navigation the Pole Star can be used to find north. Although the stars are continually on the move, the Pole Star never strays further than $2\frac{1}{2}°$ from true north. It is easily found from the position of The Plough or Great Bear (*see fig. 52*).

6 If you have the misfortune to lose your compass, a rough guide to true north can be found by using your watch and the direction of the sun. Hold the watch flat and point the hour hand at the sun. Bisect the angle between the hour hand and twelve o'clock. This direction is south (*see fig. 53*).

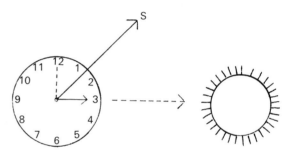

Fig. 53 Finding north by using a watch

7 Altimeters can be very useful to provide an extra point of reference, the exact height above sea level, but they have disadvantages.

—Altimeters are expensive and they are an extra item to carry.

—They are fragile and delicate instruments which are easily damaged.

—They work off barometric pressure thus they are very susceptible to weather changes. They must be reset at regular intervals from positions of known spot height.

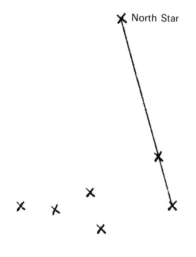

Fig. 52 The North Star

7 Mountain Safety

Mountaineering is an adventurous sport and as with similar sports such as canoeing, sailing, caving, motor racing and hang gliding, there is an element of risk. If you are not prepared to accept this fact you had better stay at home and become an armchair mountaineer.

What we as mountaineers can do is to minimize the risk by making correct decisions at the right time, by using the correct equipment and by taking avoiding action if danger arrives. A racing car driver does not develop his skills by reading books or by sitting as a passenger in a Grand Prix car, he learns from active experience on the track. In the same way actual practical experience on the hills and rock faces in all weather conditions leads to a far deeper knowledge and understanding of mountain craft than can be gleaned from books or films. Of course books and films can make an important contribution to mountain safety, and serving an apprenticeship on the hills under a competent leader is extremely valuable, but there is no substitute for first-hand knowledge. Leading a rock climb is a vastly different experience from acting as second man, likewise having to make the decisions as the leader of a party of hill walkers makes for rapid maturity. After a few years of regular mountaineering activity you get into the habit of assessing the countless variables that must be evaluated before making a decision. The process becomes automatic, rather like driving a car along a busy street.

When I first started mountaineering I tended to be slapdash and over optimistic. I remember getting lost in the mist on as mild a mountain as Ingleborough in Yorkshire because I couldn't be bothered to take a compass. On another occasion I refused to believe the compass and descended from Scafell Pike to Eskdale rather than Borrowdale. I have suffered cold hands, hunger and many a soaking because my equipment was not up to standard. But I have learnt from my mistakes and my arrogance and now I am a far safer climber.

It is in the first few years of a mountaineer's active life that he is most vulnerable to accidents. Statistics provided by the Mountain Rescue Committee of Great Britain show that in 1978 there were 276 accidents on the hills of Britain involving physical injury, including 37 fatalities. But to see these figures in perspective we must appreciate that a very large number of walkers and climbers are active on the hills. The latest estimates which are compiled by the Countryside Commission and are used by the British Mountaineering Council are 600,000 hill walkers and 60,000 rock climbers. The trend in mountain accidents over the last 16 years is most interesting (*see fig. 54*).

The number of climbing accidents has shown only a very small increase in spite of the enormous growth in the popularity of rock climbing as a sport, and the rise in the standard of routes being climbed. In 1963 the Joe Brown era was at an end and the climbing world was gathering itself ready for another great assault on rock climbing standards. This it achieved but still the push continues upwards and nobody knows where it will end. It is all the more remarkable that the climbing accident total has kept fairly constant. I can see two main reasons to explain this.

Firstly, there has been a vast improvement in the quality of safety equipment and, through the media, manufacturers have brought their products to the notice of climbers. Only very rarely do you see irresponsible climbers fooling around on rock faces with sub-standard equipment and poor technique. Secondly, expert tuition is available to young climbers at many mountaineering centres which are run, and heavily subsidized, by local Education Authorities and the Sports Council.

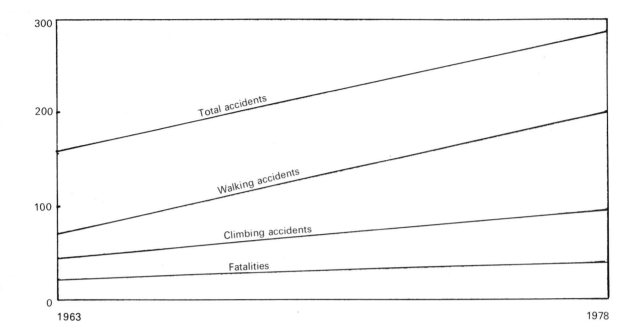

300

200

100

0

Total accidents

Walking accidents

Climbing accidents

Fatalities

1963   1978

Fig. 54 Trends in mountain accidents

Nevertheless rock climbing accidents when they occur are still very serious, this is clearly illustrated by the fact that they account for roughly half the annual total of fatalities.

The gradual rise in the total number of hill walking accidents gives less cause for satisfaction although minor accidents, such as broken arms and ankles, will be closely related to the number of walkers out on the hills. Evidently walkers still get lost in the mountains, they still venture out unfit and ill-equipped and they make wrong decisions. It is encouraging that the percentage of fatal accidents to hill walkers has steadily decreased over the years. Again this reduction is due to better training and equipment, and much greater general awareness of particular hazards such as hypothermia.

The Mountain Leadership Training Board has been very active in running courses for party leaders and climbing instructors. Mountain Leadership Certificates have been awarded to climbers satisfying the Board as to their competency to take young people into the mountains. Candidates were required to pass a week's assessment course which was most stringent and demanding; in addition they had to show proof of a minimum number of completed mountaineering expeditions and be holders of a valid First Aid Certificate.

Following the tragic accident in the Cairngorms in 1973, when a party of Edinburgh school children perished in a blizzard, there was pressure from Local Authorities and headmasters for their mountain leaders to take the MLC qualification. Many teachers did so and many failed, but a considerable number just opted out of the responsibility of taking children to the hills.

Recently the Mountain Leadership Training Board has come under a good deal of criticism from the British Mountaineering Council. The BMC feels that the possession of an MLC does not necessarily mean that the leader is safe on the mountains with a party of novices and thus the certificate is not worth awarding. A compromise has now been reached between the BMC and the MLTB whereby far more weight is attached to the experience of the candidate. The candidate's log book of expeditions undertaken is thoroughly scrutinized by the examiners and provided that it shows broad mountaineering experience under varying conditions and also provided he has passed the weeks's assessment course, his log book is endorsed with a stamp of competency as a mountain walking leader. More advanced qualifications are the Instructor's Certificate and the Instructor's Advanced Certificate. Of course even with the log book endorsement a leader could still make mistakes, we all could, but the qualification guarantees a certain minimum level of competence in the hills. Don't let us drive away our mountain leaders; it is a responsible and often thankless task that they perform and they bring tremendous pleasure and the opening up of new horizons to their charges.

Before setting out

1 Study the map and try to familiarize yourself with the main features of the area.

2 Plan your route carefully, bearing in mind the hours of daylight and the strength of the party. Allow a wide safety margin.

3 Leave behind, with a responsible adult, details of the intended route, the names of the party and the expected time of return. If you are leaving a car unattended for more than 24 hours, leave a note in the window.

4 Obtain an up-to-date weather forecast.

5 Check that every member of the party has the correct equipment and that it is actually packed in his rucksack.

6 Make sure that certain items of safety equipment for the party as a whole are being carried. Such items are:

First-aid kit	Emergency bivvy bag or
Length of rope	lightweight tent
Whistle	Map and compass
	Emergency rations

On the hills

If you are a member of a small group you will not need to appoint a leader to make the decisions. You will be able to discuss the route together and the pace will settle down to accommodate everyone. You will be able to move far and fast, and the options open to you will be much greater.

At the start of your mountaineering career though you will need to gain experience by joining larger parties under the watchful eye of a mountaineering instructor. You will be expected to co-operate fully and immediately

with the wishes of the leader, although you will be quite free to ask questions and discuss his decisions.

The leader's responsibilities are varied and exacting.

1 He must take the lead, choose the route and select the actual line to be taken over the mountains.

2 He must keep the party together at all times and therefore he must walk at the pace of the slowest. A 'back marker' should be appointed to stay at the rear and inform the leader if the party is becoming strung out. He should make regular counts to ensure that nobody is missing.

I remember descending Mam Soul in the remote western Highlands late one November afternoon when a boy in my party stopped to tie up a boot lace. We were 1000 feet above a wide col where there was a patch of level grass so I told him to meet us there. Half an hour passed and he had not arrived so we set out in haste and panic to sweep search the area. I blew the whistle and we all shouted, and finally we found him just before darkness fell. He had become disorientated and hopelessly lost. It was a remote and barren region and I was sick with anxiety; if we had not found him I should have been forced to walk ten miles to Cluanie Inn to call out the rescue services.

3 He must not be influenced by pressure from other members of his party. If he has made the decision to turn back before reaching the summit, perhaps through lack of time, fatigue or bad weather, he must not retract in spite of the disappointment caused. Again, he must decide where and when to stop for rests and for lunch, and he must ensure that it is he alone who determines the length of the break so that schedules are kept.

4 He must supervise the passage of tricky sections of the route such as pitches of rock scrambling and river crossings, and he must decide whether or not to use the rope. On steep and loose ground he must remind the party of the dangers of rock fall.

5 He should keep a wary eye on the weather and he should have some knowledge of meteorology to predict an approaching storm.

6 He must know exactly what to do in the event of an accident and a knowledge of basic first aid would be invaluable.

7 In cold and wet conditions he must constantly be on the look out for symptoms of hypothermia amongst the members of his party.

8 On return to base he must report his safe arrival and if, following a change of plan, he returns to a different place he must immediately report by telephone to prevent the possible call out of the rescue services.

Mountain hazards

Hypothermia
The Mountain Rescue Committee's annual accident report for 1976, a typical year, showed that the most common injuries sustained on the mountains were:

Hypothermia	55 cases
Head injuries	46 cases
Fractured ankle	34 cases

In the wet and cold climate of Great Britain hypothermia is a major hazard. It is a condition resulting from severe chilling of the body surface with reduction in body heat. Wet clothing provides poor insulation from the cold and in a strong wind the rapid rate of evaporation quickly cools the body surface. Children lose heat very rapidly and they are particularly susceptible. Exhaustion and low morale can also contribute to the advance of hypothermia.

Thus we would expect a party of fit climbers who are in good spirits and are well insulated from the wet and cold to be unlikely to suffer from hypothermia. Nevertheless in bad weather you should be constantly on the look out for the signs of approaching hypothermia which are:

—Severe uncontrolled shivering which is the body's attempt to supply sufficient blood to the skin when the core temperature of the body falls below 36°C.
—Lack of co-ordination of limbs.
—Uncharacteristic behaviour.

35 Outcrop climbing in Staffordshire. (Photograph by John Woodhouse)

—Slow thinking, slurred speech or disturbed vision.
—Loss of consciousness. This condition is very serious indeed because it means that the core temperature has fallen so low that the brain is being starved of blood.

It is not easy to treat hypothermia cases in exposed situations high up in the mountains so it is much better to avoid the condition at all costs. At the first indication that all is not well with a member of the party you should:

—Give him energy-giving foods such as sweet tea or glucose tablets.
—Ensure that he is wearing adequate clothing including anorak, gloves and balaclava.
—Redistribute his rucksack load amongst the rest of the party.
—Proceed down to the valley with all possible speed.

If the condition of the sufferer does not improve you must take immediate action. Erect the tent and place him in a sleeping bag together with a companion to provide body warmth. To raise morale light the stove and make tea for everyone. Alcohol should not be given because it can cause a surge of blood to the skin, the blood then cools rapidly before being returned to the heart where it further lowers the core temperature.

If you have no tent or sleeping bag, find a sheltered place behind a rock or a wall or, failing this, build a windbreak. Place the person inside a polythene bivvy bag which is well insulated from the ground and attempt to keep him as warm as possible. Meanwhile send for help immediately and treat the case as a full accident alert. Should a doctor or trained medical assistant not be available at base, the person should be rewarmed by immersion in a hot bath. The safe heat of the bath water can be gauged by insertion of your elbow.

River crossings
Let us consider an imaginary situation. It is a day of unsettled weather but the morning starts fine and you decide to set off to climb a remote peak in the heart of the mountains. Soon after leaving base you cross a stream dryshod by boulder hopping. An amusing incident occurs when one of your companions slips on a wet stone and gets a foot wet, but

you have saved a three-mile detour to the nearest bridge.

By lunch time steady rain has set in but you don your waterproofs and feel determined to bag your peak. The rain, wind and poor visibility slow down your progress but eventually you all reach the tiny cairn marking the summit. There is no view and it is far too cold to linger so you turn about, face the gale and struggle down the now saturated hillside to the valley. Wet and weary you squelch your way back to base dreaming of a hot bath and a substantial supper.

The stream which you crossed with ease a few hours before is now a swollen, turbulent mass of brown water filling the banks and hurtling towards the sea. But the idea of an extra three-mile walk to the bridge is unthinkable so you gingerly begin to wade across the stream. The water rises over your knees and the force of it tries to pluck your feet from the stream bed but you are nearly half-way across and, encouraged by your companions, you decide to continue. In mid-stream you stumble, fail to regain your balance, and fall headlong into the torrent. Your waterproof suit fills with water, your rucksack bears you down, you lose all sense of direction and within minutes you have drowned.

A horrific story but one that is only too common in the mountains. Drowning accidents are avoidable and thus are even more tragic than those resulting from objective dangers such as rock fall, avalanches and hidden crevasses.

Following two nasty river crossing incidents in which I was involved some years ago, I have treated them with the utmost circumspection. On the first occasion my wife Trisha and I, together with friends, Alan and Janet, were mountain camping in the remote Knoydart peninsula in the western Highlands. For four days in mid-March we had enjoyed perfect sunny weather; we had climbed mountains, bathed in Loch Hourn and camped in high and delectable places. The last day was to be relatively easy, a high ridge, a descent to the glen and a walk back to the car.

We woke to the sound of rain and wind buffeting the tent and we quickly packed up camp and struggled on over the tops in lashing rain and sleet, which numbed our bodies and soaked us to the skin. We stumbled down to the glen with the rain sweeping down in curtains and the hillsides white with foam. The path lay alongside the north edge of Loch Quoich but on rounding a corner, we were confronted by the Amhain Cosaidh burn. It was a foaming, roaring torrent fully 50 yards across, swirling into Loch Quoich. The top branches of trees were sticking out of the water and beyond, tantalizingly, we could see our path continuing.

Our only chance lay in striking up the glen beside the burn until we should be able to cross. As the daylight faded we struggled on for three miles but to no avail, the rain never eased and with our leaden packs we became exhausted. My arms were suffering from pins and needles and my legs were numb – symptoms, I now realize, of advancing hypothermia. Our last gingerbread had sufficed for breakfast and lunch some hours before. Ahead of us a stag swam across the river with just its antlers visible above the water.

Eventually, safeguarded by the rope, Alan managed to cross the river, Janet attempted to follow but was swept away only to be played back to the bank by the rope. Alan crossed back and with great difficulty we erected a tent, pegs were useless in the sodden ground so we put huge boulders on the guys. Even so, at regular intervals the guy ropes were snapping like cotton, the gale was so severe. We crawled into our sodden sleeping bags and, shivering uncontrollably, we somehow survived the night. The tent saved our lives. By morning the burn was down and we were able to make a crossing.

My second river epic occurred in Iceland where the rivers are unbridged, swift and laden with sediment from the ice-caps. A boy in my party, without my knowledge, attempted to wade across a wide and foaming river. He was swept away and half drowned before we managed to pull him to safety. Although he recovered quickly he was badly shocked and it had been a salutary lesson to us all.

Before attempting a river crossing you must observe the following rules:

1 If in doubt about the safety of a crossing don't attempt it. Walk to the nearest bridge or wait for the floods to subside.

2 Walk along the bank to find the shallowest stretch.

3 Use an ice axe or stick as a third leg.

4 Never remove boots.

5 Always use a safety rope and make your attempted crossing downstream from the anchor point.

6 Shuffle your feet along the bouldery river bed to find the best footholds.

7 Face upstream so that the force of the water is not acting behind your knees.

8 If a crossing is unavoidable and no rope is available, the party should stand one behind the other in a line facing upstream and shuffle across sideways.

Lightning

To be caught in a severe electrical storm when climbing a high peak can be a terrifying experience. Your hair may literally stand on end, your ice axe hum and your hands tingle.

Since the electrical discharge passes to earth by the shortest route possible, the summits of mountains, ridges and rock projections are the most vulnerable to a strike. If you take shelter up against a rock face you may receive the currents running to earth and you will be in the line of fire of displaced rocks from above. The safest place to sit out an electrical storm is out in the open away from large boulders or pinnacles of rock. Contrary to popular belief, there is no need to discard your ice axe.

Benightment

However well you plan your mountaineering days and attempt to allow for every eventuality, sooner or later you will suffer benightment. On difficult ground it is safer to sit out the night rather than to blunder about in the darkness. With modern equipment you should be able to survive the night, even in winter time, without too much discomfort.

In 1953 the crack German climber Hermann Buhl spent the night standing on a narrow ledge at over 26,000 feet without proper bivouac equipment, food or water following his lone ascent of Nanga Parbat. Another remarkable bivouac was achieved by Dougal Haston and Doug Scott in 1975 when they survived the night in a snow cave without oxygen at 28,700 feet on Mount Everest.

When you have decided that an emergency bivouac is going to be necessary, you should use the remaining hours of daylight to descend as far as possible, then you should look for shelter from the wind, a lee slope, a bluff of rock or a hollow will do or, failing that, you must build a wall of stones. Try to keep up the morale of the party and keep them occupied. Collect heather and bracken to insulate the cold ground. Put on dry clothes next to the skin followed by all the spare clothing that you have with you. Get into your polythene bivvy bags or place your feet in your rucksacks, pulling the extensions as far up as possible. Divide the remaining food into portions and eat small amounts at regular intervals.

If you are forced to bivouac above the snowline it is worth trying to construct a snow hole. Find a bank of deep, well-compacted snow from which you can dig out a large chamber. Dig with ice axes, 'dead man' snow belays or skis and even spoons can be put to use in an emergency. Since warm air rises you should build a shelf which is higher than the entrance and use it for sleeping on. Insulate your body from the snow by all possible means, the rope, rucksacks, pieces of paper and even ice axes can all be used.

In severe blizzard conditions snow holes can be life-savers but they are not easy to build and practice in their construction is highly advisable.

In very cold weather you must be on the look-out for symptoms of frost-bite. Feet are particularly vulnerable and at the first sign of numbness boots should be removed and the toes rubbed to restore circulation. If the skin is white and dead the feet should be placed on a companion's stomach underneath his clothing so that his body warmth can be utilized.

A bivouac is never comfortable but don't lose heart if one becomes necessary, provided that you remain dry and keep cheerful you will come to no harm.

In the event of an accident

If an accident should occur to a member of your party you must act decisively and immediately. Speed is of paramount importance, every second counts, so you must not dither nor panic but carry out the correct accident procedure.

Make the person as comfortable as possible. He will almost certainly be suffering from shock so he should be kept warm and well insulated from the ground. In bad weather exposure could be an additional hazard. Bandage open wounds firmly to stop bleeding and if the person is unconscious check that his airway is clear and he can breathe freely.

Summon help by giving the International Alpine Distress Signal. This is six blasts on a whistle or shouts, or flashes of a torch, followed by a pause of a minute and then a repetition of the signal. The answering signal is three blasts followed by a minute's pause. Don't wait for help to arrive, there may not be any other climbers in the area to hear your signals, so send two of your party to raise the alarm. If the route down to the valley is simple send the fastest and fittest members of the party but if the route is tricky you must go yourself. The other members of your party must stay with the casualty and you should keep them usefully occupied by building windbreaks, erecting the tent, making a brew, constructing a marker cairn and, on steep ground, tying off a fixed rope to aid the rescue team.

The climber who has gone for help must make for the nearest habitation, telephone or road. The mountain rescue services are alerted by the Police, so 999 should be dialled. It is essential that the following information be given to the Police.

—Time of accident
—Place of accident: a detailed description plus the six-figure map reference
—An indication of the type and extent of the injuries
—The name of the casualty
—The number of other members of the party

The climber should wait by the telephone for the rescue team to pick him up, and he must then guide them to the scene of the accident. In misty weather or darkness it can be a very difficult task to find an injured climber and it is vital that the position is marked by a cairn or a brightly coloured garment.

Climbing accidents are newsworthy and they attract a lot of attendant publicity. For this reason you might be tempted to evacuate an injured climber yourself. Unless the injuries are very superficial and you are near a road, this practice is not to be recommended. The inexpert handling of an injured climber can cause rapid deterioration in his condition and for spinal or head injuries it could prove fatal. It is an exhausting and time-consuming task to carry a body over rough and steep ground, and you could endanger other members of the party. Many rescues can be very quickly and effectively accomplished by use of a helicopter and a slow evacuation by hand is denying the casualty the immediate specialized medical treatment that he probably needs.

The Mountain Rescue Committee

In Britain the Mountain Rescue Committee is the organizing body for the various rescue services. Each area of mountain and moorland country has its own rescue team which can be called out at any time of the day or night. The teams are composed of local climbers who know the area thoroughly, and they hold regular training sessions to practise rescue techniques. The Mountain Rescue Posts hold the specialized equipment such as stretchers, radio sets and medical supplies which are used on the rescues. They also maintain boxes of rescue equipment at certain strategic sites in the mountains. If necessary, outside help can be called upon to provide additional assistance and expertise such as dogs trained for avalanche rescue or helicopters.

The RAF mountain rescue teams are very highly mobile and they will usually turn out to reinforce the local services. Coastguards will co-ordinate rescues on sea cliffs.

The media has always been highly critical of mountain climbers and the way they expect to be rescued by other climbers when they get into difficulties. But, in my experience, climbers turn out willingly and immediately to assist in rescues and I have never noticed any bitterness or resentment.

Many years ago I was climbing in the Llanberis Pass in north Wales when Chris Briggs, the leader of the local mountain rescue team, drove up the road and fired a red flare. Climbers descended in swarms from the crags and very soon a rescue team was organized. We carried down a walker with severe spinal injuries who had slipped on rocks near the summit of Moel Siabod and had fallen 200 feet. I remember being astonished at the difficulties in manhandling this person over rough ground even when six men were carrying the stretcher. A ten-minute stint on the ropes was quite enough.

The second rescue with which I assisted took place on Y-Garn when five minutes after I had taken the photograph on page 62 a man fell through that very cornice and broke his back.

First aid

Although there is no substitute for a proper training in first aid, it may be that the layman finds himself in the mountains, on his own, having to cope to the best of his ability with an injured climber. Here are some very fundamental instructions for him to observe before the doctor arrives.

1 If the spine is injured, the person must not be moved. Indications of spinal injury are back pain, inability to use legs and deformation.

2 Difficulty in breathing can indicate a respiratory obstruction. Check that the tongue has not fallen back and turn the head to one side to keep the airway clear.

3 Stop bleeding by tightly bandaging wounds.

4 Immobilize broken limbs to prevent movement. Ice axe shafts, fence posts and rucksack frames can be used. A broken femur is a very serious injury because of the large amount of internal bleeding and the resultant shock.

5 Treat for shock by keeping the person as warm, comfortable and happy as possible.

6 If you suspect pelvic, abdominal or head injuries do not give drinks.

Heart massage and mouth-to-mouth resuscitation are very important treatments but they should not be attempted by the untrained. It is a good thing for all active climbers to take at least some elementary instruction in first aid as provided by the Red Cross Society, or the St John's Ambulance Brigade.

8 Alpine Climbing

During the summer months climbers from all over the world congregate in the Alps, the playground of Europe, to pit their skills against the mountains. The tigers camp below the great north faces waiting for settled weather before attempting climbs which will tax their stamina and ability to the utmost. Less ambitious climbers traverse the ridges and glaciers from hut to hut soaking up the sunshine and enjoying the local fare.

The measure of a climber's ability has always been taken as the number and quality of his Alpine routes. For the average climber these will be the classic routes up the principal mountains but for the expert climber, they will be first ascents of new routes or first British ascents. To achieve the six great north faces of the Alps is the aim of every Alpine climber. Gaston Rebuffat, the crack French guide, listed these as the north faces of the Eiger, Dru, Grandes Jorasses, Matterhorn, Cime Grande and the north-east Face of the Badile. Such routes which are long and dangerous are known as *Grandes Courses*.

Perhaps the most demanding climbs of all are the great north faces in winter conditions. These first sprung to prominence in 1967 when a team, led by the American climber John Harlin, laid seige to the Direct Route on the Eiger north face. Harlin was tragically killed during the climb when a frayed rope snapped. Dougal Haston, who was a member of the team, successfully completed the route but was himself killed by an avalanche when skiing in Switzerland ten years later.

The dramatic rise in climbing standards in the Alps is reflected too in the Himalayas. Feats like Messner and Habeler's ascent of Everest without oxygen and the climbing of severe routes at high altitude by small expeditions, independent of large back-up organizations, would not have been dreamed of twenty years

ago. The Alps can offer almost every type of climbing from Chamonix granite and Italian dolomite to the major snow and ice routes of the Pennine Alps or Bernese Oberland. Similarly Austria offers the mountaineer a wide choice of countless magnificent routes of slightly lesser difficulty.

Mountaineering as a sport, rather than a solely utilitarian exercise, started in the Alps in the mid-nineteenth century. This resulted in an enthusiastic group of mountaineers founding the British Alpine Club in 1857. Yet in Britain the sport of rock climbing did not begin for another thirty years, 1886 marking the first ascent of Napes Needle on Great Gable by W.P. Haskett-Smith.

For many mountaineers Alpine climbing is a way of life. They live for the summer season when they return to their favourite camp sites, huts or hotels. The cow bells, the wine, the scent of the meadows, the burning sun on the glaciers and above all the familiar outline of the hills, these are an important part of the Alpine experience. Climbs at home become training climbs for the Alps rather than ends in themselves. To understand what the Alps mean to mountaineers you cannot do better than read the classics of Alpine literature by Whymper, Frank Smythe, Geoffrey Winthrop-Young, Hermann Buhl, Heinrich Harrer and Gervasutti. For the present-day response to Alpine climbing read the *Alpine Journal* published annually by the Alpine Club, 74 South Audley Street, London W1Y 5FF.

Although Alpine climbing is a most delightful pastime it is different and distinctly more dangerous than climbing on lesser ranges. To attempt even quite moderate routes in the Alps requires a knowledge of the full range of mountaineering skills and some ability at rock and snow climbing. Above all, because of the height of the mountains and the length of the climbs, it demands speed and fitness.

Your first Alpine season

My advice for your first Alpine season can be summed up in one word – 'Caution'. When you go to the Alps for the first time you will be confronted with new mountaineering experiences and hazards. You will meet crevasses, potential avalanche danger, loose rock and the effects of altitude and if you are too ambitious, you may expose yourself to unnecessary risk. A close shave is a very shattering experience and may destroy your confidence, hence your pleasure in climbing, for the entire holiday.

In the early days of Alpine climbing visitors to the Alps, as a matter of course, hired guides to lead them up the peaks. Learning the special Alpine techniques from a guide is the best possible way because guides undergo long apprenticeships before being awarded their coveted badges and they are men of immense experience and ability. Although I have never climbed with a guide, I have watched them in action. They move effortlessly up the rocks selecting the best route for their client, encouraging and coaxing at every step. Woe betide anyone who crosses a guide's rope, causes rocks to fall or impedes his client in any way. Guides can still be hired at the principal climbing centres but their charges are high and you may prefer to learn from a friend who has gained experience himself over several Alpine seasons. But if you and your companions cannot get help or guidance from others, don't dismay, you can launch out yourselves on modest routes.

My first Alpine season, after one year at university, was fairly typical of the inexperienced and impecunious climber. The club meet was held at Arolla in the Vallais Alps of Switzerland. But the hard men of the club had considered Arolla too tame for their aspirations and had gone to Chamonix, leaving a group of Alpine novices to fend for themselves.

Our first problem lay with the guide book. It was written in French and caused much hilarity before we managed to sort out the meaning. Nowadays this problem need not arise since several good translations are published in English. However the grading system of routes is quite different from English guide books and grades refer to the over-all standard including such factors as height, length of climb and objective dangers. The grades are:

Facile (F)
Peu Difficile (PD)
Assez Difficile (AD)
Difficile (D)
Très Difficile (TD)
Extrêmement Difficile (ED)

Individual pitches are graded by the Roman numerals I to VI, corresponding roughly to our British grades Moderate to Very Severe.

Alpine peaks are usually too high to be climbed directly from the valley in a single day and huts or cabins are used as launching pads. Many Alpine huts are in magnificent situations, built on rocky spurs overlooking peaks and glaciers, and 3000 feet or 4000 feet above the valley floor. Several hours hard grind is necessary to reach the huts. The narrow paths wind up the lower slopes of the mountains, first up through sweet-smelling pine forests and then across flower-studded Alpine meadows. At intervals you may find benches for you to rest on and perhaps a chalet selling cold milk, for huts are not just used by climbers seeking accommodation but also by walkers and ramblers enjoying a day on the easier slopes of the mountains. The paths are often marked by red-painted boulders, sometimes bearing numbers which indicate the distance away of the huts in hours walking time. At the start of your holiday, before you are properly fit and acclimatized, you will do well to meet these guide book times to huts. They are for a strong party and do not include stops.

Most of the larger huts have guardians who serve simple meals or cook provisions provided by the climbers. The guardian allocates accommodation on long wooden bunks where everyone lies together side by side on horse hair mattresses. You stretch out in your clothes and pull blankets over your head to try and muffle the snorts and grunts of the other occupants of the dormitory. The blankets are marked *Fussende* (Foot End) and *Kopfende* (Head End) to minimize the odour of old socks. I never manage to sleep well in an Alpine hut. Altitude is not conducive to sleep, nor is stuffiness, but it is the thought of the early wakening for the 'Alpine Start' that is the

chief worry. At 3.00 a.m., or earlier, the guardian comes in to report on the weather and the climbing prospects. Most climbers will admit to times when they have hoped for a bad report so that they could drop off to sleep again.

An early start is vital in the Alps because twelve- and fourteen-hour days are common. You may have 5000 feet of difficult climbing ahead of you and benightments are always serious. By mid-morning the hot sun has turned the snow to pudding and has melted

36 An Alpine hut. Sciora in the Bregaglia. (Photograph by J. Hartley)

the ice on the rock faces, causing avalanches and stone fall. But before dawn the snow is hard and crystalline and, wearing crampons, rapid progress can be made.

On my first Alpine season we stayed first at the Vignette Hut above Arolla and left at 4.00 a.m. for the Pigne d'Arolla. The party of Germans just ahead of us were led by a guide carrying a storm lantern. The hiss of the lantern and the crunch of boots on the frozen snow were the only sounds to be heard. The sun rose and reddened the snow, and our early morning headaches and nausea vanished. That day we climbed the Pigne without difficulty and by mid-morning we were back at the hut soaking up the sun on the balcony and enjoying a bottle of wine. A perfect introduction to Alpine climbing.

Later that holiday we incurred the wrath of the guardian of the Berthol Hut when we passed over a packet of porridge oats to be cooked for breakfast. The Berthol Hut stands on a buttress of rock 200 feet above the glacier. To obtain water, snow must be winched up from the glacier in a bucket and then melted in the hut, an arduous and expensive task. We had not realized that the French, German and Italian climbers make do with a continental breakfast of bread and coffee which takes little water. It is the best policy to bring simple rations for Alpine climbs. Local cheese, bread and cooked sausage make excellent lunches with spaghetti and savoury sauce for the evening meal. Water bottles are essential for, at altitude, the air is dry and the rate of transpiration high.

As we knocked off the easy peaks, the Pigne, the Aiguille de la Tsa and the Evêque, we gained confidence and began to recognize crevassed areas of the glaciers by indentations in the snow and slight alterations in texture. We abseiled the loose rock sections as a matter of course and as our fitness and confidence increased so did our enjoyment of Alpine climbing. But it was always startling to hear the low rumble of avalanches coming down the big faces and to see the billowing clouds of powder snow rising into the air – they were a constant reminder that we were amongst a major range of mountains. The giant peaks of Mont Blanc, the Matterhorn, Monte Rosa and the Weisshorn were easily recognizable and they looked most formidable.

The weather during the 1959 season in the Alps was mostly exceptionally fine but we were given a fright on the Dent Blanche by a rapidly approaching storm. On occasions in the Alps storm clouds can accumulate and a severe electric storm develop all within an hour. We were descending the south ridge of the Dent Blanche when thick clouds materialized from nowhere, the temperature dropped and snow flakes began to fall. Luckily we were just about off the ridge proper and the ground was not difficult. With ice axes buzzing we hastened down towards the tiny Rossier Hut on the upper slopes of the glacier but soon became lost. If we strayed too far down the glacier we would meet an area of gaping crevasses and a complex ice fall. In near white-out conditions with visibility little more than 10 metres, our position was becoming precarious when a grey shape loomed over us. It was the hut and our shouts brought out the guardian who lowered us a rope for assistance up the last 100 feet of steep ice.

By next morning the storm had passed, leaving blue skies and sunshine but the mountains were transformed. The rocks were plastered white and it would be at least two days before they came into conditions suitable for climbing. We returned to Arolla, stocked up with food, and walked over the Col de Tsa de Tsan into Italy, no sign of border guards at this altitude, and we stayed at the tiny Refugio d'Aosta. The little wooden refuge had no guardian and we cooked on our own stoves and enjoyed perfect peace in this most tranquil of settings amongst a carpet of edelweiss.

The next morning we dragged ourselves out of bed at 2.30 a.m. to climb the Dent d'Hérens. From the Tieffmatten Col the route was mixed rock, snow and ice and it absorbed all our attention. Steep cliffs and snow faces plunged down in all directions and although the guide book grade was only *AD*, it was for us a major climb. Sitting on the pointed summit surrounded by the most glorious views imaginable, we felt ecstatically happy and proud.

Back at Arolla the club meet began to disperse but my brother, Christopher, and I decided to stay on for a few more days and visit Zermatt. We packed the tent and heavy equipment, and sent it to Zermatt by Post Bus, a quick and efficient service. Up to the Berthol Hut for one night and then across the Col d'Hérens and down to Schönbuhl under the Zmutt ridge of the Matterhorn. By 4.00 p.m. we were sitting in one of Zermatt's cosy restaurants tucking into a huge slab of Schwarzwälder Kirschtorte. Zermatt, the mountaineer's Mecca, is perhaps

the most beautiful of all Alpine villages. It has
a fairy tale quality and the ancient charm still
remains. Old chalets, white-washed churches
and tasteful new hotels are linked by narrow
and twisting streets but, above all, it is the lack
of motorized traffic which makes Zermatt
unique. Visitors must leave their cars down the
valley at St Niklaus and proceed to Zermatt by
train. A taxi service is provided from the
station by brightly painted traps pulled by
ponies wearing bells on their harnesses. As you
walk up the streets band music wafts out of the
café windows and outside the Monte Rosa
Hotel the guides sit smoking on a low wall,
their traditional meeting place.

The stupendous peak of the Matterhorn
dominates Zermatt, it towers over the village
dwarfing all other topographical features;
Ruskin likened it to a rearing horse.
Christopher and I strained our necks gazing up
at the sparkling hanging glaciers and snow
fields; we were highly excited and began to
discuss the possibility of an attempt on
Switzerland's most famous peak. One of the
most challenging routes up the Matterhorn is
the Zmutt ridge above Schönbuhl but in 1959

38 The Dent d'Hérens from Col de Tsa de Tsan, Swiss
Alps.

the route was very icy and had claimed the
lives of two Cambridge undergraduates. From
our adjacent view point on the Dent d'Hérens
we had watched a party of guides removing
the bodies from the glacier on a sledge. Having
rejected the Zmutt, we were left with the
ordinary route up the Hörnli ridge which is
reasonably straightforward but crowded in the
summer season.

The following afternoon, spurning the cable
car to Schwarzsee, we raced up the zig-zags to
the Hörnli Hut and, along with several guided
parties, squeezed inside its dark interior. British
notions of fair play are unknown in Swiss
mountain huts and it was late into the night
before our packet of spaghetti was cooked by
the guardian. The guardian and the Zermatt
guides were thick as thieves and the guides
expected preferential treatment for themselves
and their clients.

After a dreadful night packed on a narrow
bunk designed to take half our number, we
were thankful to leave the hut at 3.30 a.m.
and, by torch light, to begin work on the ridge.
Loose rock and the antics of the other climbers

37 Hörnli ridge of Matterhorn. (Photograph by G. Lacey)

were the main obstacles to our progress. The guides would literally bar our way ahead with their ice axes and we suffered torrents of abuse as we nipped past their scrabbling and incompetent clients. Such is the cachet following an ascent of the Matterhorn that many people, who by no stretch of the imagination could be called mountaineers, pay large sums of money to guides in order to be hauled up the mountain.

Dawn broke and in the better light we progressed rapidly. Well before the emergency refuge, the Solvay Hut, we were ahead of all the other parties and after negotiating a treacherously icy section where the route deviates onto the north face, we arrived at the twin summits at 6.45 a.m. It was an intensely cold dawn, too cold to linger, but the early mists were beginning to dissolve in the heat of the sun and we had glimpses of blue sky above and green meadows far below. A couple of photographs and some chocolate, then we turned for home . . . . Mindful of the tragic descent which befell Whymper's party in 1865 when four members plunged to their deaths, we exercised the utmost caution on the way down. Nevertheless we made excellent speed over the loose screes and at 1.30 p.m., after nearly 10,000 feet of descent, we were back at Zermatt railway station sitting in the train bound for the Rhone Valley, Paris and London. So ended my first Alpine season. The Alps had broadened my experience and increased my confidence, and my expectations of Alpine climbing had been surpassed.

You do not need to attempt hard and dangerous routes to get pleasure from the Alps. You need competence and motivation and the mountains will provide the reward. In the Alps perhaps more than anywhere else the mountaineer must compromise between the challenge of the climb and the appreciation of the natural beauty of the scene. The entirely physical approach is to reach the mountain summit by a long and severe climb with nerves shattered, heart pounding and lungs bursting only to leave immediately for the valley, the day's work done. The alternative, aesthetic approach, is to find an easier route to the summit and to arrive, nervous system intact, with enough time to drink in the scene and to savour one's unique position in space.

On the one side we have the hard north face men and on the other the mountain walkers. Having veered at times in each direction, I have settled down somewhere between the two extremes; you are free to make your own choice guided by your own particular bias.

Special factors in Alpine climbing

I have already emphasized the need for caution during your first Alpine season. This is because of the many new problems which will confront you when tackling significantly higher mountains than you have been accustomed to at home. The margin of safety is less and mistakes can be much more serious, and for these reasons some new techniques and safeguards must be learned. Although, for climbing major Alpine routes, much sophisticated equipment is now available and certain highly effective but involved mountain rescue techniques can be employed, in this chapter I shall keep by advice as simple as possible.

Fitness
Make sure you are as fit as possible before you leave for the Alps. Fitness speeds up the process of acclimatization to altitude and it is a pity to waste the first week of an all too short Alpine holiday in achieving this physical state when some long mountain walks, or some runs back home in the evenings, will produce the same result.

Alpine climbs are long, even when starting out from an intermediate hut, and fourteen-hour days are not uncommon. If you are fit you will not only enjoy the climbing much more but you will recover your strength more rapidly and be able to attempt several different climbs on consecutive days from the same hut.

Speed and fitness can extract you from potentially dangerous situations. Emergency bivouacs should be avoided at all costs and you can often reach the safety of the hut in the face of an approaching storm or benightment even if you need to cross wide glaciers through exhausting deep, soft snow.

Equipment
The enormous contrast in temperature between hot sun reflected off the glacier and the sub-

zero conditions in the heart of a storm means that careful selection of equipment is vital. You cannot afford to be short of the necessary emergency gear nor can you afford to carry a heavy and unwieldly rucksack.

Down provides the ideal answer. It is light, compressible and exceptionally warm. A duvet jacket and a polythene bivvy sack should see you through most eventualities, otherwise the mountaineering gear suitable for Scottish winter climbing, as indicated in Chapter 4, will suffice. Boots should be stiff enough to take crampons and to be used for rock climbing.

Never be without ice axe, crampons, pitons, hammer and abseil slings. Even rock routes can quickly become iced up or verglassed and short alloy axes are best used here. Other essential items for Alpine climbing are map, compass, guide book, torch, emergency rations, snow goggles, extendable rucksack, water bottle, safety helmet and glacier cream to protect the skin from ultra-violet rays.

Rope technique
When your party is moving across a glacier or up a fairly simple ridge the individuals should be roped together in groups of four. The intervals between climbers should be about 4 or 5 metres with the slack held in coils as described in Chapter 3. This is the traditional Alpine method of providing safeguards for the climbers. It is a compromise between solo climbing and direct belay climbing when only one climber moves at a time, the others being securely belayed to the rock. The chief advantage of the Alpine method is speed since all the climbers move together, but for hard

39 The superb Alpine ridge of Piz Palu, Switzerland. The climber is Roger Putnam.

pitches or obvious dangers such as the crossing of snow bridges over crevasses, the foolproof single movement technique should be adopted. If much direct belaying is going to be necessary the party should be split into ropes of two when the much faster technique of leading through can be used.

If one of the party should fall down a rock face, snow slope or into a hidden crevasse the other members must plunge their axes deep into the snow and hang on tight or brace themselves against the rocks. In all probability the victim will be held before he has gained very much momentum.

Abseil pitches are common in the Alps and it is essential to know the technique thoroughly and never to compromise on the correct drill. Double check the anchor point, the sling and the karabiners and remember that you must never run a nylon climbing rope directly through a nylon belay loop. Check too that the rope runs free or else precious time may be wasted in trying to pull the rope through from the lower stance.

Crevasses and ice falls

Glaciers move slowly down towards the valleys but they are unable to hold the same contours as the ground over which they move. As a consequence the ice splits into cracks called crevasses and in extreme cases, where the ground is very steep, the ice becomes contorted into a chaos of pinnacles or seracs and deep fissures forming an ice fall. Ice falls are always treacherous and are best avoided at all costs. Crevasses too are often dangerous and they are sometimes too numerous and widespread to circumvent. However firm and solid a glacier seems to be underfoot you must always rope up. I know the rope is a nuisance and the temptation to leave it coiled up around your shoulders is great, but crevasses are often hidden under a thin covering of snow, sometimes without any outward visible signs.

Walk up the middle of the glacier where there are likely to be fewer crevasses. Look out for indentations in the snow or changes in texture and where crevasses are visible, extend them to either side with an imaginary line. Make sure you are proceeding at right angles to the general line of crevasses and not parallel to them. If in doubt prod the snow with your ice

axe. When you do meet a crevasse try to detour round; this is by far the safest method. If this proves impossible look for a snow bridge or a narrowing of the crevasse where it can be jumped. But snow bridges are often unreliable and weak, especially after the sun has warmed them, and narrow sections are often edged with overhanging lips of snow or cornices. Extreme care is necessary. Move cautiously over the bridge, on your stomach to distribute your weight if the bridge is thin, while you are belayed by the other party members.

If you do have the misfortune to fall into a deep crevasse, even if you are held on the rope, your predicament could be serious. When walking on a glacier, tie a small loop in the main climbing rope about 1 foot from your waist band using an overhand knot or a figure of eight knot. You must also carry a sling and karabiner round your neck. Now if you find yourself suspended in space inside a crevasse of cavernous depths you can quickly clip the sling and karabiner into the loop of rope which is at about chest level. Kneel or stand in the sling to relieve the constriction on your chest caused by the waist loop riding up. Such constriction has been known to cause death.

A large party may be able to extricate a fellow climber from a crevasse using a direct pull on the rope but the task is never easy. The rope cuts into the lip of the crevasse producing enormous friction. The problem is made simpler if the party above have a second rope since a loop can be lowered to the victim who, by transferring his weight from one rope to another, can be hoisted up stepwise. But if the victim is unconscious and the party is small it is far better for one member to go for help immediately. A trained mountain rescue team can use one of several crevasse rescue techniques which are described in advanced manuals.

As you leave the edge of a glacier to continue climbing on rocks you may meet a bergschrund. Bergschrunds are fissures caused by glacier ice melting away from a rock face and they can be exceptionally wide and deep. Again try to find a place where the ice does meet the rock or where the bergschrund is

40 A bergschrund in the Alps.

narrow enough to be stepped across. If all else
fails you can sometimes climb or abseil down
into the bergschrund and then climb up the
other side.

Avalanches and stone fall
In Chapter 3 I warned you to look out for
avalanche conditions resulting from fresh
powder snow, heavy deep snow or wind slab.
Certain snow slopes have a bad reputation for
avalanche danger and the wisest course of
action in the Alps is to seek advice from hut
guardians and mountain guides. Their intimate
knowledge of the mountains includes the
potential avalanche danger of the various
routes and they will be glad to help and advise
you.

Many Alpine routes involve climbing rock faces
and ridges on loose and doubtful rock. Stone
fall is always a threat and safety helmets must
be worn at all times. Keep well away from
other parties climbing above you.
Unfortunately there are some climbers who
have no thought for those below, as they tear
away at loose boulders with their hands and
scrabble with their feet.

9 Schoolboys to the Himalayas

This is an account of the first ever British school expedition to the Himalayas.

We watched hypnotized as a massive rock, the size of a double-decker bus, slowly toppled over, slid down a band of snow, accelerated and smashed to pieces before sweeping down the central couloir and finally coming to rest on the glacier 2000 feet below us. We were belayed on a rib of rock to the right of the couloir 30 metres away, but the sulphurous fumes drifted up into our nostrils and we sighed with relief. I suppose at that point we should have turned back. After all, we were only a school party and I had Charles, Simon and Patrick in my care, sixth formers aged 17 and 18 years old. But another three or four rope lengths would see us to the summit ridge, and after eighteen months' planning and intensive training, we could not admit defeat; besides which I would have had a mutiny on my hands.

We were climbing the south face of Kolahoi, a beautiful pyramid of rock in Kashmir, 17,900-feet high. Our party of thirteen was from Ampleforth College in Yorkshire. I had two assistant leaders, a doctor and nine boys chosen from over sixty applicants from the school.

Base camp was on the moraines below the northern glacier snout of Kolahoi, two days' journey for our caravan of ten ponies up the idyllic Lidder Valley from Pahalgam. This valley is rightly described as one of the most beautiful in the world. Steep slopes of giant spruce and pine; meadows carpeted with gentians and edelweiss; marmots, monkeys, kingfishers, hoopoes, bee-eaters and eagles. It was unforgettable.

We had acclimatized for a week and had succeeded in finding a route which avoided the main ice fall by ascending the eastern glacier. Camp 1 was on the east glacier at 12,500 feet and camp 2 was tucked under the long east ridge of Kolahoi at 14,500 feet. The entire expedition had helped to establish camp 2, carrying loads up 2000 feet of steep crevassed ice, which tested technique to the limit. The week which we had spent practising snow and ice climbing in the Cairngorms in March was invaluable.

My hopes of erecting two small tents at camp 3 at the very bottom of the south face had had to be abandoned. The snow at the base of the face was littered with avalanche debris and recently fallen stones. Thus I had decided to launch the assault from camp 2.

I had cut two days off our planned schedule for several reasons. Firstly, the weather had been fine for four days running and I did not think the spell could last. Secondly, we were so excited and mentally geared up for the climb that no one was sleeping and we were physically deteriorating at a great rate. Thirdly, the food situation at camp 2 was desperate. We had not brought any staple food from England and had not been able to buy convenience food in Kashmir. The camp 2 rations comprised three-day-old chupatties, cooked at base camp by Ram, our Indian cook, porridge, biscuits and Kendal Mint Cake. Nutri-nuggets of concentrated artificial protein were inedible unless curried and our pressure cooker was at base camp, so we could not cook rice. And growing boys need large meals at regular intervals.

On the night of 20 July I do not think any of us slept at all, and at midnight we listened in awe to the roar of an avalanche coming down the north face of Kolahoi. It was with great relief that we heard the alarm clock at 3.00 a.m. Staying in our sleeping bags we cooked porridge and tea, and then emerged into the cold to strap on crampons and rope up.

The glacier was frozen hard and a mess tin tobogganed away down the snow tinkling as it

41 Camp 2 on the Kolahoi glacier.

accelerated towards the ice fall. The stars gave enough light for us to see Kolahoi looming above as we cramponed up the slopes in silence. Soon after 5.00 a.m. the sun burst over the horizon and we came to life. It was a golden dawn and the Himalayas were spread out to the east as far as the eye could see from Kishtwar to Ladakh and Tibet. Dominating the skyline was the giant 23,500-foot Nun Kun only 50 miles away.

Climbing in two ropes, Charles and myself, and Simon with Patrick, it took fifteen long pitches up the rock to reach the summit ridge. The south face was exposed to the sun's rays from dawn, and although we started up the rocks at 7.00 a.m. the stones had already begun to fall. We had felt pleased with ourselves as we perched on the lower ledges above the bergschrund to take off our crampons. In spite of two and a half hours cramponing up to about 16,000 feet, we had not noticed the altitude. As soon as we started rock climbing, however, and began using hands and arms, we suffered the well-documented symptoms. Heaving and gasping, we struggled up the pitches hardly conscious of the stones winging down over our heads or the magnificent panorama of peaks coming into view behind neighbouring Bur Dalau and Buttress Peak.

Along with most British climbers abroad we felt at home on the rock, in spite of the horrible looseness, for most of our training had been on Yorkshire outcrops and in north Wales. We preferred to find routes up smooth slabs of rock which, although steeper, were at least sound. There were plenty of placements for nut runners and we were entirely engrossed in the climbing, but time was slipping by. It was 11 a.m. when we completed the final (hardest) pitch at grade IV and paused on the summit ridge for some biscuits. The exposure was monumental; 7000 feet down the sheer north face we could just make out the orange base camp tents. Charles announced that he was going to be sick – the half-cooked porridge prepared at 3.00 a.m. had not agreed with him.

The true summit was a snow cornice 500 feet along the razor-sharp ridge. The ridge itself was composed of slivers of rock stuck in at crazy angles and holds could not be trusted. Dislodged rocks would crash down on either side and bound down to the glaciers in a most unnerving way. At intervals there were overhanging pinnacles or gendarmes which had to be traversed, making the climbing distinctly tricky. I kept an open mind but at that moment I did not really think we could go any further on Kolahoi.

We took off our rucksacks and secured them to a rock and drank some water. Everyone was very tired and had there been a suggestion of turning back I would have complied immediately. But there was no question of retreat. To leave rucksacks on a summit ridge and to proceed without them is by most accepted mountaineering practice an act of folly, but high mountains cannot always be climbed by keeping strictly to the rules, and experience and instinct are more important. I do know that we were sufficiently stretched by the climbing to take any action that would increase our balance and freedom of movement. Our ultimate success, so precariously gained, might not have been possible if we had kept our rucksacks on our backs.

'My lead', said Charles and started to move towards a horribly steep snow gully under the first gendarme. His footsteps crumbled away and he retreated. Charles then descended for 30 feet and moved on to two rocks which protruded up through the snow. The rope was almost directly above him giving good protection. The rocks held. Thus we by-passed the gendarme and this airy and dangerous pitch proved to be the hardest on the summit ridge. . . . At 1.30 p.m., after six pitches along the ridge, we assembled at the last rock belay before the snow cap. Individually we kicked steps to the top of the cornice and planted a small Union Jack (after all it was Jubilee Year) but we were far too exhausted to feel much elation. Monsoon clouds had built up in the north denying us the distant views of Nanga Parbat and K2.

We were far behind schedule and foremost in our minds was the thought of the return along the ridge and then down the unending and loose south face. It is to the great credit of the boys that without delay we turned round and climbed down steadily for six hours non-stop until we reached the glacier. No one put a foot wrong. The first down on each rope left runners to protect the last man. In general we preferred to climb down rather than abseil since it would have been time-consuming to find secure abseil points or cracks for pitons, although we did abseil the last pitch before the glacier. Dashing down the glacier in a rope of four and jumping crevasses we reached camp 2 in near darkness at 8.30 p.m., having been climbing for sixteen hours. Unfortunately there was no welcome for us at camp 2 for we had made our climb two days earlier than expected. The main party was down at base camp enjoying goat curry and duty-free whisky. Wearily we melted snow for tea and forced down leathery chupatties and jam.

Throughout the entire expedition there was no bitterness, envy or jockeying for the lead and the boys were always cheerful and co-operative. Volunteers for load carrying were always forthcoming. In this way a school expedition scores over an adult team of ambitious climbers, although there are disadvantages. The boys have limited experience and one has to be constantly on the look-out for careless belays, balled-up crampons and other safety points which adult parties can take for granted. On the south face of Kolahoi though we were climbing as equals and the three boys realized that their lives

42 Two ropes of schoolboy climbers leaving for camp 2 on Kolahoi.

depended on their own ability. They responded to the challenge and they will never forget the experience.

So much for our ascent of Kolahoi, but you are probably asking the question: 'What on earth was he doing in the Himalayas with a party of relatively inexperienced schoolboy climbers?' This question is best answered by considering the special factors involved in Himalayan climbing, the planning, training, selection of peak and the rewards of climbing in the world's greatest range.

A member of a Himalayan expedition is never solely concerned with the climbing problems which confront him. He must overcome the problems of altitude, uncomfortable living conditions and physical debility. He must play his part as a member of a team, do his share of load carrying and bear the annoyances of living cheek by jowl with his fellow climbers. Before he tackles the actual peak he will have endured an exhausting approach march through the foothills with, possibly, recalcitrant porters, monsoon rains and an aching gut from the unhygienic conditions. But the mountaineer gladly accepts these deprivations plus the

considerable financial cost and the months or years of planning to enjoy the privilege of being a Himalayan climber. Indeed they are a part of the Himalayan experience.

It is only the large and prestigious Himalayan expeditions which get the publicity. Expeditions to Everest, K2 and Kangchenjunga make the headlines, but every year there are dozens of smaller expeditions to lesser peaks in the Great Himalayan Chain. If I could find a modest peak in the Himalayas that was reasonably accessible, surely I could take a party of skilled young climbers to attempt it, I mused. In previous years I had led school expeditions to the Iceland Ice Caps and the Trollaskagi Mountains of northern Iceland, the High Atlas Mountains of Morocco and the peaks of the Lyngen Peninsula in Arctic Norway. Following my experiences on these mountains I had developed a high regard for the ability and responsibility of schoolboy climbers.

Mountaineering interest flourished in the school and in 1975 a particularly keen and talented nucleus of climbers moved up into the sixth form. These were boys who had never

43 Charles Morton on the summit snow cap of Kolahoi.

missed a club meet and who had proved themselves on Scottish snow and ice, and on Welsh rock. My thoughts turned to the Himalayas and I sought a suitable peak.

Our experience was necessarily limited, as is the case with all school parties, and the margin of safety would have to be wide. The mountain must not be too high nor too inaccessible, yet it should provide us with an approach march through the foothills, several glacier camps and some serious climbing – the three ingredients of all Himalayan expeditions.

School holidays are short so we could not afford to spend long periods acclimatizing or trapped, storm-bound, in tents. Permission from the authorities must be readily forthcoming for we could not undertake detailed planning and training only to be denied access at the last moment.

Planning the expedition

Many of the factors that we had to consider when planning our expedition to the Himalayas are common to all expeditions. If, when you have sufficient experience on other (lesser) ranges of mountains, you are considering an expedition to the Himalayas yourself you will find these details useful. We received plenty of advice, some of it misleading, and we made many mistakes but luckily none serious enough to jeopardize the success or enjoyment of the expedition.

The experience of India was in itself traumatic. None of our party of thirteen had previously been to the sub-continent and our difficulties in coming to terms with the alien environment were very real. Expeditions should proceed to base camp in the mountains with all possible speed before they are weakened and demoralized by the heat and unhygienic conditions of the valleys and plains.

In the school holiday period of July and August the central and eastern sections of the Great Himalayan Chain are blotted out by the monsoon, leaving only parts of Kashmir in north-west India and the Karakoram in Pakistan which are suitable for climbing. In the mid-1970s the Indian government was beginning to open Kashmir to foreign expeditions following years of closure after the border clashes with China and Pakistan.

Kashmir seemed ideal for our purpose because the country is spectacularly beautiful and it is easily accessible by air from Delhi. Lord Hunt recommended a peak called Kolahoi, an impressive rock tooth known locally as Gwashi Bror, the Goddess of Light. Kolahoi was 17,900-feet high and had been first climbed in 1911 by Neve and Mason at the third attempt. Lord Hunt had climbed the south face of Kolahoi in 1935, since when it had had several other ascents.

The route to Kolahoi lay 26 miles up the Lidder Valley from the village of Pahalgam in the Himalayan foothills and 70 miles from Srinagar, the capital of Kashmir. It seemed an ideal objective. The approach march of two days would not eat into our tight schedule, the height should not pose too many problems of acclimatization and logistics (three camps above base should suffice) and the climbing would be challenging but free, I hoped, of too many objective dangers.

I was fully aware of the potential hazards of acute mountain sickness (AMS), particularly with schoolboys. Pulmonary Oedema can occur below 18,000 feet unless precautions are taken and this fear, together with the probable incidence of sickness and diarrhoea, convinced me that we must include a doctor in the party. It was essential that the health of the boys was safeguarded and a doctor would relieve me of the medical responsibilities, leaving me free to concentrate on the climbing. A recent survey by John Winter (*Alpine Journal* 1976) had shown that if a rate of ascent of no more than 220 metres per day is rigidly adhered to above 2500 metres, everyone should escape AMS. We planned our acclimatization on this basis.

Dr Yves Dias was by far the oldest member of the party, at 54 years, but he was one of the fittest and he made more load carries up to camp 1 than any other expedition member. In the event we had no trouble with AMS but sickness and diarrhoea afflicted us all below base camp level in spite of using water purification tablets and avoiding salads and fruit.

It is all too easy to fall prey to disease and infection when visiting India. We underwent a course of immunization and vaccination against smallpox, typhoid, paratyphoid, tetanus, cholera, yellow fever, poliomyelitis and

44 Kolahoi as seen from the north.

hepatitis. Daily doses of the anti-malarial drug Paludrin and the anti-dysentery Sulphatriad were taken. Not all these precautions are obligatory to enter India but they are highly advisable.

It was a red letter day when permission to attempt Kolahoi was granted by the Indian Mountaineering Foundation and half the fee of 2000 rupees was waived. At our request Mr K.K. Sharma had been deputed as official Liaison Officer. 'KK' had been recommended to us by a previous expedition to Kashmir and we were exceptionally lucky to secure the services of so charming and helpful a man. 'KK' met us off the plane at Srinagar and remained with us throughout our stay in Kashmir. He organized the ponies and pony wallahs, cook and camp assistant, and the transport to Pahalgam. He was a knowledgeable mountaineer and helped carry supplies to camps 1 and 2. Accompanying Liaison Officers are compulsory for Himalayan expeditions and an unco-operative man, unwilling to help in ironing out local problems, would seriously effect the morale and efficiency of an expedition.

By now it was clear that the expedition was viable and further plans could proceed, but would there be any response from boys in the school? A preliminary notice produced the overwhelming response of sixty firm applications to join the expedition. Who can say that the spirit of adventure in the young is dead?

We had been advised that a small party would be best because they could make on the spot arrangements in India for such things as buses, pony and porter hire and accommodation. Our final party numbered thirteen and was made up of three leaders, the doctor and nine boys. The selection of the lucky nine was a heart-searching job. We looked for mountaineering experience, fitness and compatibility and the time spent on deliberations was worthwhile for, although there were disappointments for the unlucky boys, the selected nine lived fully up to our expectations of them. We were never once let down by lack of co-operation or determination.

Plans gathered pace. We received 'approval' from the Young Explorers Trust, the screening panel for expeditions of young people and in February I was delighted to hear that I had been awarded a Winston Churchill Memorial Trust Fellowship as leader of the expedition. Air India offered us bargain fares from London to Delhi and then on to Srinagar. From Srinagar we would proceed to the mountains by local bus and then pony train. We needed to arrive at base camp in good fettle and that meant hiring ponies, not only for the main bulk of food and equipment but for our personal luggage too. We also needed the best drugs available and sound insurance policies. Equipment was expensive and had to be of top quality, I could not risk the party's safety by buying cheap ropes, tents and clothing. Besides, we planned to leave some equipment in Kashmir with the Education Department, to help the mountaineering courses run by 'KK'.

Forecast costs rose alarmingly to £7000 and to keep the individual contributions down to an acceptable figure we launched an appeal for half this sum. Appealing for money is by far the most distasteful part of an expedition as well as being enormously time-consuming. Literally thousands of letters were written and we reached the target just two days before leaving Britain. The £7000 forecast turned out to be an under-estimate and the breakdown given below might be of interest to future expeditions.

Income	£
Parents' contributions	1000
Industry	1300
Everest lecture by John Scott	100
Raffle	700
Sale of inscribed pens	200
Sponsored log collection for Senior Citizens	200
	3500
Members' contributions	4750
TOTAL	8250

Expenditure	£
Travel	4000
Expenses in India	1000
Equipment	2600
Overheads, insurance, permits etc.	400
Report	250
TOTAL	8250

Food

I had decided early on in the planning of the expedition that we would take all our baggage and provisions with us on the flight to Delhi. I had read too many accounts of expeditions being delayed for weeks in Delhi trying to get stores, which had been sent early by air freight, released from warehouses at the airport. We intended to buy all our food in Kashmir but, for special high altitude use only, we bought Kendal Mint Cake, 'One Cup' soup sachets and lemonade powder with us from England. In order to meet the stringent baggage allowance of 20 kilos per person considerable 'hand luggage' needed to be taken on to the plane. In addition, anorak pockets were stuffed with heavy items such as pitons, hammers and tent pegs. Wearing boots, snow gaiters, balaclavas, sweaters and anoraks we found Heathrow Airport on a sultry July morning to be stifling and we looked like Michelin men as we waddled into the departure lounge, Charles leaving a trail of oxtail soup powder in his wake.

It was a serious mistake to assume that we could buy palatable European-type food in Kashmir. Together with 'KK' and Ram, our Indian cook, we shopped as best we could in the fly-infested stores of Old Srinagar but the bulk of our purchases were far from ideal. Oats, rice, flour, biscuits, cooking oil, spices, jam, tea and dried milk made up the staple diet. Fruit and fresh vegetables were abundant and cheap because the Vale of Kashmir is sheltered, well irrigated and extremely fertile. At base camp we retained the services of the most reliable ponyman, Azizmir, to journey down to Pahalgam at regular intervals in order to post the mail and replenish food supplies.

Meat was poor, butcher shops were horrific and in the heat the meat turned bad within hours. Later on in the expedition we bought eggs, chicken, sheep and goats from the local shepherds, called *gujars*, who were pasturing their flocks in the Lidder Valley.

Yellow vegetable curry and chupatties were our main sustenance both at base camp and further up the mountain. It was the job of old Azizmir to keep the fire going with scrub juniper roots and dried thistles, and he would squat for hours, wrapped in his blanket keeping some indescribable potion bubbling in the cooking pot. To watch Ram expertly making chupatties was an education. With a flat wooden tray, rolling pin, flour and water and an old car hubcap set over a Primus stove as a griddle he could turn them out at the rate of one a minute. It was not unusual for Ram to make one hundred chupatties in a day. We ate chupatties with curries, with fried eggs on top and with sardines and when spread with jam and rolled up like sausages, they were delicious.

More or less continuous supplies of tea were available at base camp and each day started at 7.00 a.m. with the cry of 'Morning, Chai', from Ram as he served tea at the mouth of the tent. Dehydration is always a problem at altitude and it was a struggle to approach Yves' target intake of 6 litres of fluid per day, particularly at the higher camps when snow had to be melted for water.

But lack of appetite is a common symptom of altitude and most expeditions make sure that there is ample tasty food readily available in the high camps. Our diet of leathery chupatties and porridge at camp 2 was just not sufficiently nourishing for the job on hand and had we been delayed in camp by bad weather, the expedition would surely have failed.

Training

About half the boys selected for the expedition had had previous climbing experience on rock and ice. Several of them were, even at the age of 17, quite competent mountaineers. But everyone needed to be thoroughly acquainted with the skills and techniques of mountaineering, for everyone would be required to carry supplies up to camp 2 at 15,000 feet.

It is not easy to cope with steep and crevassed ice slopes when you have a heavy load on your back, you are puffing and panting from the rarified atmosphere and the glare of the sun off the glacier is giving you a blinding headache. The Himalayas are not the range to discover that your cramponing technique is wanting or to tangle the rope. A delay caused by incompetence can be a frustrating experience on a low crag but it could prove serious on a major peak.

Having selected the team, we had twelve months in which to prepare the boys for the climb. At Ampleforth we are extremely fortunate in having, only a few miles away, several outcrops suitable for rock climbing. We had a choice of gritstone or rather loose limestone and the latter prepared us, unknowingly, for the appalling looseness of the south face of Kolahoi. In addition to regular sessions on these outcrops we made week-end visits to the Lake District and north Wales for practice on the easier classic rock routes and a highlight was a half-term trip to the Cuillin of Skye.

Training on snow and ice took place in the

133

45 Charles Morton on the summit ridge of Kolahoi.

Easter holidays on Lochnagar in the Cairngorms. We were lucky to find the 1200-foot cliffs liberally plastered with snow and ice and we gained valuable practice in step cutting, cramponing and surmounting cornices. The weather was ideal for our purpose and our equipment was fully tested. The Highlands were in the grip of an exceptionally cold polar air stream and days alternated between clear blue skies with biting wind and full snow blizzards. We were camping in Glen Muick and every night the burns were stilled with ice and mornings and evenings found us in duvet jackets stamping around in the snow wrestling with the Primuses. These conditions were a good deal more severe than any we encountered on Kolahoi, and the spirit and determination of the party bode well for the big test to come later in the year.

Three of the boys, Charles, Simon and Patrick, were outstanding climbers. I could rely completely on their skill and judgement and it was these three who succeeded in conquering Kolahoi after that unforgettable sixteen-hour climb of 21 July 1977. Following our successful assault on Kolahoi I was quite sure in my

mind that no other members of the party had the ability and experience to succeed, and for this reason I had to break the news to the rest of the expedition that there would be no further attempts on the mountain. I was very conscious of the grave disappointment this would cause but in the event I was wrong. Without exception the remaining six boys admitted to being relieved at not being asked to join the assault team. It was enough for them, they confessed, to be climbing in the world's number one range and to have reached a height of 15,000 feet after a determined and difficult struggle.

Conclusion

Having read the above, very brief account, of our own minor expedition, I am sure you realize that an expedition to the Himalayas is not to be undertaken lightly. But don't be discouraged, the rewards far outweigh the mammoth effort of planning the expedition. I am sure you will find, as we did, that once at base camp many of the problems are left behind and you can concentrate on the job in hand, the climbing of mountains which, after all, do not greatly differ the world over.

Index